THE **Bark Busters**™ GUIDE
to Dog Behaviour and Training

THE **Bark Busters**™ GUIDE
to Dog Behaviour and Training

Sylvia Wilson

SIMON & SCHUSTER
AUSTRALIA

First published in Australia in 2003 by
Simon & Schuster (Australia) Pty Limited
20 Barcoo Street, East Roseville NSW 2069

A Viacom Company
Sydney New York London Toronto

This edition specially printed for Bark Busters Inc.

Visit our website at www.simonsaysaustralia.com.au

National Library of Australia
Cataloguing-in-Publication data

Wilson, Sylvia
The bark busters guide to dog behaviour and training.

Includes index.
ISBN 0-6840-2087-4

1. Dogs – Training. 2. Dogs – Behaviour. I. Title.

636.70835

Bark Busters™ is a registered trademark.
Cover design by Avril Makula
Illustrations by Ian Faulkner
Internal design by Peter Guo, Letter Spaced
Typesetting by Peter Guo, Letter Spaced
Typeset in Sabon 11.5 pt on 18 pt
Manufactured in the United States of America

10 9 8 7 6 5 4 3 2 1

Contents

Foreword

When I met Sylvia, I had been living an unbearable life with very little meaning. My world had shrunk to a very uninteresting place, and I was always running around in circles, chasing my tail, never knowing which way to turn.

I vividly remember meeting Sylvia. The day was hot and sultry and I was all strung out and stressed again. This feeling of being out of control had started to overwhelm me. I had lost the ability to communicate with the people around me and no longer had any friends. They had all grown up and moved on to enjoy their lives, while I couldn't get my life together.

You have probably realised by now that I'm a dog – in fact, a handsome male German Shepherd called Tonka.

My friends down at the park had told me all about Sylvia. It was love at first sight. I considered myself to be rather good-looking, although young and inexperienced. Sylvia obviously saw some potential in me that no else could see. She believed that I could live a normal, happy life, and through patience and understanding she made me whole again. Sylvia's gentle touch made me feel alive and gave me a purpose. I am no longer spinning out of control. Sylvia Wilson, you're a wizard.

Tonka (German shepherd, aged 9 months)

Acknowledgments

My sincere thanks and appreciation is extended to the following people: my beloved husband Danny, whose love, support and neverending faith in me made this book possible. The wind beneath my wings.

To my dearly departed parents, Eddie and Lily, who put up with a precocious child who brought home stray after stray. They always believed that one day I would have a career that involved working with dogs.

To my children, Brett and Donna, who both work for Bark Busters™, Donna at headquarters in Australia (Donna was the official photographer for this book) and Brett, who is assisting the United States operation. They will hopefully one day carry on the Bark Busters™ empire.

To my dearly departed friend, Jean Higgenbottom, an expert in her own right, who truly believed in me and taught me to believe in myself. I have no doubt that she is here by my side assisting me. Thanks, Jean, you are not forgotten.

To the RSPCA, for giving me the opportunity to know so many great dogs during my nine-and-a-half years in charge of the South Coast New South Wales branch. My years with them gave me an invaluable insight into dogs' behaviour as well as the ability to perfect my techniques.

To my friend Doug Malouf, who shares my deep love of dogs, who long ago planted the seed by saying, 'Sylvia, you must write a book'. Thanks, Doug.

To all the Bark Busters™ therapists throughout the world, this is your book and I thank you for having faith in the company and in helping us to spread the Bark Busters™ philosophy throughout the world and for your love and dedication to all dogs.

rate your dog's behavior at www.barkbusters.com

Introduction

Many of the common problems experienced by dog and puppy owners in today's society would be preventable if prospective dog owners were better informed about what to look for when selecting a new puppy or dog.

Dogs enjoy the status of being the world's most popular pet. Even countries that once had very low rates of pet ownership, such as Japan and China, are rapidly becoming nations of passionate dog enthusiasts. Despite their popularity, dogs attract a great deal of criticism, which is generally due to human mismanagement or lack of understanding.

In our status-driven world, people are often attracted to breeds that are 'in vogue', rather than considering the manageability and temperament of a particular breed and its suitability to their life. These important factors in making a decision about a new pet often fall to the bottom of the priority list.

One of the most-surrendered breeds of dogs in recent years has been the dalmatian. This striking breed, with its white body, black spots and regal looks, became very popular when the movie *101 Dalmatians* was released. People tended to fall in love with the breed's stunning appearance, and bought one without realising that, for the uninitiated, dalmatians are a very difficult breed to train, with the result that thousands of dalmatians ended up in pounds and animal shelters, prompting the dalmatian breed clubs to come up with the slogan, '101 reasons why you shouldn't buy a dalmatian'.

In my work I regularly come across 'in vogue' dogs with very unsuitable temperaments – dogs that have difficulty coping in this fast and furious society because they don't receive the necessary leadership from their owners.

As our society has become more sophisticated and domesticated, we have lost our ancestors' understanding of dogs and their needs. My working life is spent explaining and lecturing on the way dogs think and why they react the way they do. Dog owners are often amazed by my revelations, with many people reaching the conclusion that dogs are very complex creatures. However, I find that dogs have very basic requirements and simply want to be understood by their owners.

Bark Busters™ shows you how to select the right dog for your lifestyle, how to communicate with your dog, and how to demonstrate appropriate leadership. It explains when to correct your dog's behaviour and when to give praise. Choosing the right dog and learning how to educate and communicate with it will make your life more pleasurable.

1

Finding the right puppy for you

Finding the right puppy for you is like finding the right partner in life. It can be the difference between heavenly bliss and a life full of dramas. Selecting a new puppy is one of the most important decisions you will make.

Try to avoid buying a puppy on impulse. Do your research about which breed will best suit your situation and personality. There are many books available on different breeds. See page 220 for the Bark Busters™ list of the 50 most popular breeds.

Large breeds are an unsuitable choice for small, frail people or for those living in townhouses or small apartments. Lap dogs are unsuitable for people who don't want a dog that lives inside. Researching the most suitable breed of dog for your personality and lifestyle will ensure that you have fewer problems down the track.

Some dogs that were bred for hunting or pulling sleds aren't the most suitable choice for a companion dog. Although modern breeding practices have altered many of the natural traits of these dogs, they still have some way to go. This is not to say that these breeds should not be taken as pets, but the uninitiated person may experience problems when training them.

To ascertain the most popular breeds selected for competition trialing, visit a dog trial to see the dogs competing in obedience competitions. Breeds that are commonly represented in dog trials include: German shepherds, labradors, border collies, dobermans, rottweilers, Australian shepherds, golden retrievers, Australian cattle dogs and kelpies. If you are interested in entering your dog in competitions, then one of these breeds might be the best choice. All breeds of dogs can be trained, however, some will train up better than others. For example, hunting dogs such as beagles, bassets, foxhounds, German shorthaired pointers and weimaraners can prove a challenge for the inexperienced dog owner. Similarly, sled dogs, such as samoyeds, Siberian huskies and malamutes can also prove difficult to train for the uninitiated.

Once you have determined the best breed for you, the next step is to find a reputable breeder. It is wise to look for a breeder who has been breeding the same breed for many years, rather than one who changes with the trends. Reputable breeders register their puppies with a breed registration organisation and will have wormed, vaccinated and micro-chipped their puppies.

They will be concerned about the homes that their puppies go to and will ask you a lot of questions about how you intend to house and care for the puppy.

A reputable breeder will be able to assist you with your selection of a puppy. A good breeder will have spent many hours with the puppies, watching them grow and develop, then weaning them. They will know each puppy's personality and its place in the pecking order.

In order for the breeder to help you choose the best puppy for you, provide them with as much information about yourself and your circumstances as possible. Tell the breeder about:

- the type of house you live in
- the lifestyle you enjoy
- whether you like walking or going to the beach
- whether you have children, and their ages
- whether you would like an indoor or outdoor dog
- any other dog you have and its age and sex
- whether your elderly parents live with you
- any disabilities you might have.

This information will assist the breeder with the selection of the right puppy for your needs. They will be less likely to pick the active puppy full of energy if you don't do much walking, live in a unit or have recently had knee surgery.

Choosing your puppy

Once you have determined the most suitable breed of dog for you, here are some tips for choosing your puppy. In my opinion, the most suitable dogs are the even-tempered dogs that are lower down the pecking order. They tend to present fewer problems for their owners and make great pets. Be careful not to be taken in by the sometimes cute antics of the more dominant personalities!

Three-step puppy selection

Step 1:

View the mother and father of the puppies to get an indication of the puppies' temperaments. Generally the offspring will have many of the traits of each parent. If one of the parents is unapproachable, then the chances of a puppy from that litter having the same temperament is quite high. If you discover an undesirable temperament in one of the parent dogs, it is wise to look elsewhere. Don't be tempted to look at the puppies, because you may not be able to resist taking one! It's worth the wait for a puppy with the right temperament.

Once you have viewed the parents and are quite satisfied that their temperaments are sound, move on to watch the puppies playing. The more dominant puppies will display behaviour such as biting the other puppies on the back of the neck, jumping on them, barking and pinning them to the ground. Some growling and snarling might take place. A dominant puppy will push its way in if you are patting or paying attention to its litter mates. In other words, it will be the bossy one.

Pack leaders or strong-willed personalities are not generally the right pets for the average pet owner. All dogs need strong leadership, but dominant dogs need very determined management. Generally speaking, the average person does not have the mettle for the type of constant discipline required by these stronger personality types.

Puppies that are lower down the pack order are generally more easily managed and trained. The puppy that moves out of the way or avoids confrontation will be lower down the pack order.

Once you have identified the type of puppy you are looking for, ask the breeder to separate them to another section of the yard, away from the other puppies.

Step 2:

Using a soft toy, leather wallet or glove, drop an item on the ground a few feet away from the puppies and watch for each puppy's reaction. The puppy that runs away is unsuitable and should not be chosen. This puppy is fearful and will more than likely turn into a nuisance barker down the track.

The puppy that moves away but returns quickly to investigate is fine and can be selected. It will be a cautious type, but with the correct socialising and training, will make a great pet. The puppy that immediately runs to investigate and sniff the object is also fine. Providing it's not the dominant, bossy type, it should make a very outgoing and friendly companion.

Step 3:

The final step to finding your compatible mate is to lift and hold each selected puppy in your arms. The one that sits quietly and doesn't wriggle is the one that is going to present the least amount of challenges for you.

You have now chosen the right puppy.

Summary:

- Do your research to find the right breed for you.
- Select the right breeder.
- Provide the breeder with as much information about yourself as possible.
- Follow the three-step puppy selection process.

2

Selecting the right adult dog

When acquiring a new dog, I always opt for a more mature dog that can immediately fit into my busy life, rather than a puppy. A puppy needs careful nurturing and plenty of time and energy to ensure it receives the right education and grounding. Taking on a full-grown or mature dog is a handy shortcut to getting the right dog for you.

Animal shelters are a very good source of adult dogs with even temperaments that are looking for good homes. Sometimes because of circumstances beyond the owners' control some of these dogs will have been surrendered.

Some people can't cope with being reminded of a loved one who has passed away, every time they look at their loved one's pet. Other people are unable to take the dog with them when they move house.

rate your dog's behavior at www.barkbusters.com

Of course, there are dogs that have ended up in shelters because they have behavioural problems. However, the temperament testing carried out by most animal shelters generally weeds 'problem' dogs out. At the very least, the animal shelter staff will make you aware of the problem, which, in most cases, can be fixed with training.

Breeders can be another excellent source of an adult dog. Some breeders do what is known as 'running a dog on', which means keeping a puppy to see how it turns out for showing purposes. These dogs are generally educated and socialised, and are put up for sale between six and 12 months of age. The breeder kept my doberman, Kaydee, in this way. She is the most adorable and well-behaved dog you could ever meet. At 14 months, Kaydee was already house-trained and mostly obedient when I bought her. She was a 'ready-made' pet.

Some things to consider when buying a full-grown dog:

- Will the dog readily approach you?
- Is the dog healthy?
- Is the dog friendly?
- Does it jump on you? (This is a minor problem that can be cured with training.)
- Is it good with children?
- Does it like both men and women? (Some dogs are fine with women but aloof with men. It is important that the dog likes both sexes.)
- Is it easy to manage or is it too excitable?
- Will it be too much of a handful for your children or elderly parents?
- Is it aggressive to other dogs or some humans? (Training can help, but it is preferable to get a dog that is already well behaved.)

- Is it likely to chase cats?
- Is the dog protective of food?
- Is the dog easy to groom? (This problem can also be solved with proper training.)

A dog that doesn't willingly interact with you when patted and bounds about the place sniffing is generally not the most suitable dog for a pet. Don't expect a dog to know and love you immediately, but if it doesn't have a capacity for this, its first reactions will give that away.

Choosing a mature dog

Three-step adult dog selection

Step 1

Have the owner or kennel assistant place the dog on lead for you and then spend some time with it. See how it copes with you and your children. Dogs that don't like children will try to avoid them. Some dogs will ignore the children altogether, stiffen up, or try to pull away. This type of dog will only be interested in being patted by the adult. A dog with this kind of temperament is not suitable as a family pet or for anyone who has children as visitors.

Step 2

Try walking the dog around, observing how obedient it is and how easy it is to walk on lead. A dog that pulls a little is fine, as training can fix it. Check to see if the dog will respond to basic instructions.

If the dog pulls on the lead and is unresponsive to you, ask the owner or kennel hand to walk the dog. If the dog is responsive to them, then in time it will more than likely be responsive to you, once the dog accepts you as its leader.

Step 3

Run your hands down the dog's back and watch for its reaction. Does it spin and try to stop you? This is not the sign of a well-adjusted dog. See if the dog will let you touch its feet and tail and allow you to groom it.

Ask the owner or kennel hand to help test the dog for food aggression. They will give the dog a small bowl of food to see if it displays any undesirable behaviour, such as growling or crouching down possessively over the bowl. Do not attempt to approach the dog while it is eating or allow any children to approach it. Leave this for the person who knows the dog best. Question the owner or kennel hand about the things they have noticed when the dog is eating: is it safe to stay near the dog? Does it curl its lip at you? Very careful thought should be given when selecting a dog with food aggression problems. Ask yourself the following questions:

- Will the children be at risk?
- Will guests be at risk when they visit?
- Will the family be at risk, if the dog buries a bone and someone stumbles upon it?
- Is food aggression the reason for the dog being re-housed?

Puppies also have the potential to develop these problems. However, the selection of an adult dog allows you to see these problems more easily, as they are not disguised by a puppy's cuteness.

Immunisation

Whether you buy a puppy or a full-grown dog, it is best to ensure that its immunisation is current prior to sale or several days before re-housing, as a change in the environment causes a dog to experience stress. The golden rule is not to take a dog or puppy out of its environment until several days have elapsed since it was immunised. Stress weakens the immune system of a re-housed dog, which causes many dogs to fall victim to diseases against which they were previously immunised.

Regardless of whether their coverage is not due again for a couple of months, I always ensure that my dogs' immunisation is redone at least two weeks before sending them for boarding.

I also give them a low daily dosage (500 mg) of sodium ascorbate (Vitamin C) a couple of weeks prior to boarding to boost their immune systems. Take care to give only very minute quantities (75mg) of Vitamin C to puppies as it may cause diarrhoea.

Heartworm

All dogs should be tested for heartworm, a parasitic disease that is transmitted by mosquitoes and is on the increase. Heartworm was once only contracted by dogs in tropical climates such as Queensland, but it has now spread further afield.

Puppies as young as two weeks old can be treated for heartworm. However, dogs over six months of age require a test before commencing treatment because starting an animal that already is infected on preventative treatment can prove fatal. Always consult your vet before commencing any treatment.

Micro-chipping

Micro-chipping of dogs before sale is mandatory by law in most states of Australia. The process involves the insertion of a micro-chip at skin level into the dog's neck region. The micro-chip possesses coded information unique to each dog that can be read by vets, animal welfare workers, dog rangers and other authorised personnel with a hand-held scanner. The micro-chip enables a lost dog to be reunited with its owner.

If you are buying a full-grown dog previously owned by someone else, it may already be micro-chipped. If this is the case, ensure that you receive the necessary papers for the transfer of ownership.

Registration

All dogs by law must be registered by the local council by the age of six months. If you select an adult dog, it might already have been registered with a council. If this is the case, then you will need to make sure you receive copies of the dog's registration papers in order to transfer ownership.

Summary:

- The right option for busy people may be a full-grown dog.
- Research the breed and type of dog that is best suited to your lifestyle.
- Follow the three-step selection process.
- Transfer any registration or micro-chipping into your name.

3

Nurturing your new puppy

New puppies need a great deal of nurturing. Just like new babies, they need a warm place to sleep, education, an area to romp and play, as well as several feeds per day.

Make a decision early on about where you want your puppy to sleep and whether you want your puppy to live in the house or be confined to the backyard.

An increasing number of dog owners believe that it is best to allow their puppy to sleep in the bedroom with them. This might sound fine in theory, but in practice it may lead to future problems. At Bark Busters™ we often receive calls from owners whose dogs are suffering from separation anxiety – 'the fear of being left alone'. The dogs most affected by this problem are those that have been allowed to sleep in their owner's bedroom and given around-the-clock access to them.

Problems also arise when these owners want to board their dogs during holiday periods or when the owner suddenly decides that they no longer want the dog sleeping in their room. A dog that has become accustomed to sleeping in its owner's bedroom becomes stressed and anxious once its owner is not around.

People who take over the nurturing of a puppy and overindulge it are missing a crucial element to understanding what makes dogs tick. Constant nurturing of puppies does not occur in nature. The mother dog begins to leave her brood very early in their development so that she can toilet or drink. In the wild, the mother dog also joins the other dogs on the hunt, returning with tasty morsels of food for her brood. Even a domesticated mother dog will begin to leave her litter as soon as the puppies start to grow and mature. They no longer need the constant care that newborn puppies need.

If you do decide to allow your puppy to sleep in your bedroom, then it is best to provide a den where it can sleep. A den can be a crate that is closed up at night and covered over. This is a far better option than allowing your puppy to sleep on your bed or on a rug on the floor. The puppy will become accustomed to the crate (its den) regardless of where you move it. It can also be locked in during the night, which will assist you in starting your puppy on the road to toilet training.

This method will also allow you ease of transportation, providing you with a future solution when your puppy or dog has to be 'babysat' or boarded. This gives your puppy the security of a familiar place to sleep at all times.

Naturally you will need to upgrade the size of the portable den as your puppy grows. The ideal size is a den slightly larger than your puppy and just big enough for your dog to stand up and turn around. This will prevent your puppy or dog from fouling the den and will encourage good toilet habits. Puppies and dogs will not generally foul their sleeping quarters.

Ensure that your puppy has access to fresh drinking water and is not left in the den for an unreasonable length of time. Overnight is fine, providing your puppy has been given ample opportunities to go to the toilet.

Give the puppy a soft, cuddly toy for company. If you are lucky enough to be able to implant its mother's scent on the toy, your puppy will settle down much quicker. Failing this, place your own scent on the toy by carrying it around with you for a short while before giving it to your puppy. This special soft toy should only be given to your puppy at night, as this then becomes the subliminal signal that it is bedtime.

At Bark Busters™ we believe that dogs should always be made to feel that they are part of a pack. However, in our busy society, it isn't always practical for a family to have the dog with them at all times. Deciding where your puppy should sleep from day one is therefore vitally important. Start the way you intend to go on if you want your puppy to grow into a well-adjusted and well-behaved dog. Dogs need to be part of the human/dog pack structure, but I find that puppies are best housed in a separate room from their owners and in a portable den. These days dogs have to learn to cope with a certain amount of isolation, so being left alone for periods encourages independence.

All puppies should be given some access to the house during your waking hours and at times when they can be watched, so toilet and basic training can be provided.

The problems associated with over-nurturing of puppies and dogs are highlighted in the following case history.

Case history

Stella was a much-loved and adored German shepherd puppy when her owners, Jenny and Simon, first brought her home. Being the nurturing, motherly type, Jenny decided that Stella would sleep in their bedroom and on their bed.

Stella loved this arrangement and would curl up with Jenny and Simon each night when they retired. This appeared to work well for everyone concerned for about seven months until Stella lost her puppy appeal and began to shed her winter coat. Hair began to appear everywhere. Tired of cleaning it up, they decided to put Stella outside permanently.

Stella immediately became very anxious. Not having slept outside before, the evening noises and sounds began to frighten her, and she panicked, trying to get back inside the house to be with her pack again.

She began frantically scratching at the door in an effort to be allowed back in the house. Stella's world had been completely turned upside down. She felt like she had been ostracised from the pack, and couldn't understand why.

Stella's behaviour intensified to the point where she scratched at two exterior doors, totally destroying them.

Jenny and Simon finally called Bark Busters™.

The first step was to establish Jenny and Simon as Stella's pack leaders. They had overindulged Stella, bowing to her every need. Then overnight they had reversed their pattern of behaviour, kicking her outside, and changing her sleeping quarters.

It was obvious to us that Stella had looked upon the bedroom and sleeping with the pack as her haven. She needed a new haven, a place where she could feel safe again.

We suggested that Jenny and Simon provide Stella with a portable den (a crate). This was placed near the back door and under the cover of the back veranda, with a weatherproof cover placed over it covering three sides. The entrance to Stella's den was made to face the direction of the back door. At first the front gate to the den was left open. We instructed Jenny and Simon to only lock the den in the evenings or when they were going out for short periods.

The den became a safe place close to the house where Stella could go when she was frightened. Stella was then trained to go into the den when she was anxious about noises. This was achieved by firstly creating the noises artificially and teaching her to go into the den rather than trying to get in the door.

By creating a pattern of behaviour at normal times, Stella soon learned that she could find a safe place other than the inside of the house, for those times when she was frightened. Stella's problems and fear of noise would never have occurred if she had become accustomed to being in the backyard from an early age and had the opportunity to experience all the sounds of the night. She would have learned very quickly that these noises couldn't hurt her.

Once you have established the area where you intend your puppy or dog to sleep, you need to spend some time training it to go to that area. If outside, ensure that the area you have selected is close to the house. No dog wants to be isolated way up the back of the yard. Dogs will refuse to go into kennels, either because they are too far away from the house, or they do not accept them as their special place.

A portable crate or den is an appropriate solution as it allows for you to lock the puppy or dog inside until they become accustomed to this area as their sleeping quarters. You can the put the den anywhere you please, even outside. The den can then be left open during the day and, if adequately covered with a waterproof tarpaulin and under the cover of a veranda, your puppy or dog will be safe and warm.

Settling in

The settling-in period takes approximately two weeks. Be aware that the true nature of your new arrival will not surface until then.

Yelping and whining might occur in the first hours of settling a new puppy or dog into its den or sleeping quarters, especially if it have always been accustomed to having company. Be prepared for this. It is advisable to settle the new arrival in at least two hours before you intend to go to bed. This allows you time to discipline any unwanted behaviour when you are wide-awake. If your puppy or dog begins to whine or bark, resist the temptation to go to it because otherwise it will think that the sound it is making got your attention and it will repeat this behaviour to make you reappear.

Instead, move into earshot but not into view. Wait for your puppy to call out again then growl loudly and clap your hands. That way it won't feel abandoned but will realise that its cries won't bring the desired result. The settling-in period should only take you a couple of days, providing you do not relent and give in to your puppy's cries. Your puppy or dog should then always settle down very quickly when put to bed at night.

If using the portable den, ensure that you lock it at night to prevent your puppy from going to the toilet in the wrong place.

Diet

It is wise to do some research into canine nutrition before settling on the right diet for your puppy or dog. There are many good books available from your local bookstore on the subject of canine nutrition and what diet is best for your dog. See page 228 for recommended reading.

Preservatives, colouring and grains can create hypoactivity in some puppies and dogs, which is why it is important to find out the most appropriate diet for your breed of dog.

A young puppy requires several feeds per day. These should be small meals as overfeeding can lead to digestive upsets, colic and sometimes diarrhoea.

The dog's breeder or previous owner will be able to tell you what your new puppy or dog was previously being fed. Only feed small amounts of this food at first, increasing as the puppy settles in. Puppies have very tiny tummies and new arrivals need time to adjust.

Bones

Raw, meaty bones are very important to a dog's diet. However, during the summer months your puppy or dog should only be fed bones in the cool of the evening. Bones cause some dehydration in dogs and may dehydrate them to dangerous levels in extreme hot weather. Always supply plenty of water when feeding bones.

Chocolate

Never feed chocolate to a dog or puppy. Chocolate contains theobromine, which can prove toxic to animals. Chocolate has been responsible for the death of several dogs.

Milk

Dogs have no nutritional need for milk once weaned. Dogs receive sufficient calcium through eating bones and this calcium is more easily absorbed. Cows milk is designed for cows, which have several stomachs, not canines that only have one. Milk in a dog's diet can cause diarrhoea.

Research

In 1997, researchers at Colorado State University of Veterinary Medicine released their findings into combating cancer in canines.

They recommended excluding lactate and glucose-containing foods because cancer cells thrive on sugars and create lactate as a waste product. They reported that lactate poisons the animal by depleting its energies, thus weakening the dog. The researchers recommended limiting sugars and simple carbohydrates in a dog's diet.

The report also stated that a diet high in fat and low in simple carbohydrates enables canines suffering from cancer to survive longer. Omega–3 fatty acids were reported to reduce lactate levels and reduce or eliminate metastatic disease. Cancer cells are unable to utilise fat, which is a natural energy source for the dog.

To read more about this research, visit the website at: http://www.cancercure.colostate.edu

Grains

Many vets and animal nutritionists now agree that grains should be kept to a minimum in a dog's diet. Although the jury is still out on the subject, I believe that some grains can cause hypoactivity. I have been able to demonstrate this fact many times by eliminating grains from the diet of hyperactive dogs, resulting in a dramatic turnaround in the animals' behaviour.

The Colorado Institute Of Veterinary Medicines' 1997 research also highlights the fact that grains should only be eaten in moderation by canines. Dr Ian Billinghurst in his books *Give Your Dog A Bone* and *The BARF Diet* states that canines have no nutritional need for grains.

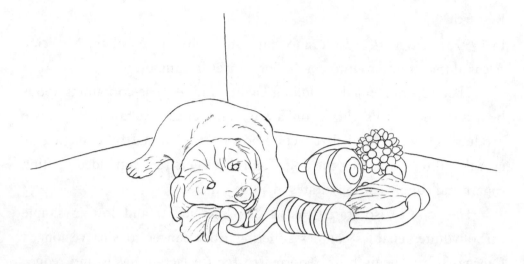

Entertainment

Once your new arrival has settled in, you will need to supply it with some form of entertainment.

There are many good quality doggy toys on the market. Be careful when selecting toys for your new charge as some toys are too easily chewed and can lodge in the dog's teeth or tummy.

The problems with sticks

Many people opt for sticks as a play item for their dog because they're a cheap option. However, a stick thrown to a dog can cause serious injury if it lands sticking up out of the ground and the dog jumps on it. Sticks have been known to become lodged under a dog's tongue, requiring an operation to remove the stick.

The problems with balls

Small balls may prove to be more of a problem for a dog or a puppy than larger ones. Dogs have been known to swallow small balls, which can become lodged in the dog's throat, once again requiring surgery for removal. One vet told me that he regularly operates to remove a tennis ball that a dog has inadvertently swallowed.

The Kong toy

There is a durable doggy toy made of rubber called a 'Kong'. It is shaped like a beehive and is extremely bouncy. The shape of this toy adds to its appeal, as it will bounce unpredictably in several different directions when thrown. It also has a hollow centre that allows for food treats, fish or meat paste to be placed inside, offering hours of fun for the dog, which tries to get at the treat to eat it.

Buster cube

Another durable and worthwhile doggy toy is the 'Buster cube'. This toy is made of strong plastic that acts as a puzzle for the dog. Food is placed inside the interlocking internal system. The dog only receives the treat when it pushes the cube in the right direction. This toy has a system for adjusting the degree of difficulty to suit the intelligence of the dog concerned.

The Buster cube provides much-needed stimulation for intelligent dogs that would otherwise be getting up to mischief to alleviate boredom. Some dogs have been known to play with these types of toys for hours, which is a far more productive pursuit than digging up their owner's flowerbeds.

Sandpits

Sandpits are another great source of entertainment for puppies and dogs, providing them with an area where they can dig, play and bury things. The sand also provides your dog with an area to lie in that is warm in the winter and cool in the summer, keeping them off your garden beds.

Sandpits are easily built just about anywhere. Simply create a boxed or bricked-in area, or dig out an area large enough for your puppy, and fill it with clean beach sand (available from most garden supply stores).

Wading pools

A child's wading pool is ideal for keeping your dog cool in summer. Place the pool in a shady spot. Your puppy or dog will enjoy hours of fun in its pool, sometimes spending the whole day just lying in the water to keep cool.

Always ensure that small children cannot get access to the pool, as they can drown very quickly in just centimetres of water.

Warnings

Do not provide any toy for a puppy that encourages any type of tugging, pulling or leaping. Items such as ropes or tyres hanging from trees can jolt the underdeveloped skeleton of young dogs, leaving them with dislocated shoulders and back problems.

If living in a wasp-infested area, be sure to only feed bones and raw meat that your dog can eat immediately. Wasps may land on meaty bones, biting a dog on the tongue and causing death by choking when the dog's tongue swells up.

Toilet training

Where puppies are concerned, one of the most frequently asked questions is about toilet training. Most people have no concept of a puppy's capabilities. Proper toilet training is very important and should be started as soon as you bring your puppy home. Puppies, like very young children, have no control over their bladder or bowels. They feel the urge and they eliminate almost immediately.

Puppies can be trained from an early age if their owner is mindful of when the puppy will need to go to the toilet and gets them to the desired spot.

To successfully toilet train a young puppy, it is helpful if you know the most likely times your puppy will need to go to the toilet:

• immediately after waking from a nap or sleep

• immediately after eating or drinking

• after exuberant play

• when you arrive home

• when your puppy is excited

• if your disciplinary actions are too harsh.

If you are aware of these times, it will assist you in toilet training your puppy or dog much faster. Firstly select an area in your backyard where you would like your puppy or new dog to toilet. It must be sunny and ample for the size of your dog, and preferably well away from the house. It should also be regularly cleared of all droppings and hosed, otherwise your dog will choose another less cluttered area.

Ensure that you always encourage your dog or puppy to this area at the times listed above and at other times when you feel it might want to relieve itself. Repeat the words, 'Go to the toilet' over and over. This will make it easier for future toilet stops as the puppy will know what this phrase means.

Of course, your puppy will need to go at other times, but if all of these times are strictly watched they will soon learn to go to the right spot or at least walk to the back door to be let out. It is up to you to ensure that you are watchful for any indications your puppy gives you that it wants to go to the toilet.

Inside-housed puppies should initially be given only limited access to the house. Start by closing off all interior doors, blocking off carpeted areas and bedrooms.

Whenever I have seen a puppy with bad toilet manners, it is because the owner has allowed the puppy free range of their house. The owners become distracted, the puppy wanders in to a bedroom or living area that is carpeted and this then becomes the toilet area. Sometimes an owner will catch their puppy in the act and then smack it for its behaviour. This only creates more serious problems, because the puppy begins to hide whenever it needs to go to the toilet.

The reason for hiding is simply the fact that puppies that are not correctly house-trained have no idea that they shouldn't toilet in the house. Just like a baby, a puppy will go off and find a spot to relieve itself when the urge takes it. When disciplined for this, the puppy becomes confused, so it hides from the owner when it needs to eliminate, leading the owner to mistakenly believe that their puppy knows it has done the wrong thing.

By using baby barricades available from baby supply shops you can block open walkways and entries to carpeted areas. Be aware that puppies will generally want to go to the toilet on carpeted areas because of the scent they hold, and accidents will happen even with the most diligent owners. When accidents do occur you should use a powder urine soaker available from most pet shops. The powder soaks up the urine while it neutralises the smell. Never smack or discipline your puppy when accidents occur. Instead, calmly pick your puppy up and take it to the designated toilet area.

I believe that puppies should be given access to the house and know their way around, but this should be done at a time when you are not busy with household chores and are available to watch your puppy. At other times, put your puppy into its portable den.

Crating

Crating is a foolproof way of toilet training a puppy. Puppies and dogs do not like to foul their sleeping area, so the crate needs to be just big enough for them to sleep in. Having used this technique many times when bringing little puppies home from the RSPCA to rear and hand feed, I recommend it highly. The crate acts as a den, which dogs naturally love. It provides a safe haven when the puppy cannot be watched, during meal times and when you are busy around the house or at night while sleeping.

Puppies will generally learn to hold on during the night if allowed to eliminate last thing before retiring.

It is wise to put your puppy to bed at least a half an hour before you go to bed yourself.

Playpens

Good puppy management is made easy with the use of a playpen. A playpen can be simply a child's playpen purchased from a baby store. These are ideal for indoor use, but ensure that a deterrent is sprayed on the wooden panels and slats to prevent any chewing.

Outdoor playpens can be created by digging posts well into the ground and enclosing with weldmesh or cyclone wire, ensuring the puppy cannot climb out.

Summary:

- New puppies need lots of attention.
- Decide early on where your puppy will sleep.
- Portable dens make great sleeping quarters.
- Correct all barking and whining in the early days, using the Bark Busters™ process.
- Conduct your own research into the right diet for your growing puppy.
- Puppies need entertainment.
- Toilet training should be started from day one. Follow the guidelines for the times your puppy will most likely need to toilet.
- Inside access to the house should be limited by using barricades to block access to carpeted areas and bedrooms.

4

Early puppy education

In the wild puppies would naturally receive their formal and ongoing education from their mothers, other 'litter mates', as well as any elders in the pack if they remained within the pack.

When you take on the responsibility of a new puppy or dog, you also take on the responsibility of that creature's education. Without their mother or members of their pack to learn from, they look to you, their owner, to show them right from wrong, and educate them in the ways of the world.

The first thing you need to know is that as a pack animal, your new puppy or dog will need a leader. That has to be you, and you will need to be consistent. Dogs view inconsistency as a sign that the pack leader is losing his or her ability to lead and that a leadership challenge should be launched.

At Bark Busters™ we say, 'Dogs won't apply for the top job if it isn't vacant'. This means that dogs won't generally challenge a consistent and firm leader.

Education starts from the first day you bring your new puppy home. Your puppy has left a structured environment where it knew its place in the pecking order. It needs to learn the rules of its new environment. You must show that you are its leader and now it must listen to *you*.

Introduce your puppy to all of the family as well as any other animals that share your property. All introductions should be carried out on lead, ensuring that you correct any undesirable behaviour from your puppy from day one.

This is your opportunity to educate your puppy, showing it how you want it to behave in its new environment. You will need to use a correction word to let your puppy know when it is making a mistake. I employ the use of a growl word for times when a puppy or dog is behaving in an undesirable way. Simply growl 'Bah' in a guttural tone when your puppy misbehaves. This growl tone immediately lets the puppy know that you are not pleased with its behaviour. Dogs instinctively respond to the growled 'Bah', unlike the more commonly used word 'No'. The dog does not instinctively comprehend the word 'No' as a misdemeanour word: it has to learn the word first, slowing the process dramatically. Meanwhile, bad habits are formed. Much faster results are achieved if you communicate your displeasure in the dog's language. Praise your puppy with 'Good boy!' in a high-pitched, melodious tone when it behaves.

A puppy's mind is like the wind blowing in all different directions at one time. A puppy will see something and run off to investigate, only to be distracted by something else that takes its interest: a leaf will move and it is off again.

The amount of time spent on your puppy's education will no doubt vary depending on whether or not your puppy is kept indoors or outdoors. A puppy that is housed indoors is a lot more work, but will learn more quickly because it receives a lot more attention. You will have to be far more diligent with a puppy that has unlimited access to the house and take into account the destruction that a young puppy can cause, as well as toilet training of that puppy.

When puppies are kept indoors they must be educated quickly and sensibly, as they have the potential to wreak havoc. This is the reason many people opt for moving their puppy outdoors. Although this might seem the easy option, it is not always the best option. Puppies housed outdoors will still create havoc, but in the garden.

Begin by limiting access to those areas where you know your puppy can cause damage.

Good puppy management

Puppies housed outdoors

The following are guidelines for housing a puppy outdoors:

- Fence off garden beds.
- Supply a playpen with shade and water.
- Move shoes up out of your puppy's reach.
- Raise the height of the clothesline.
- Roll up all garden hoses and move them out of your puppy's reach.
- Block off access to any wooden or plastic outdoor furniture.

- Pick up all children's toys.
- Supply your puppy with its own toys.

Puppies housed indoors

The following are guidelines for housing a puppy indoors:

- Close off all interior doors.
- Pick up all children's toys.
- Move all precious and breakable items.
- Block off all access to carpeted or restricted areas.
- Supply your puppy with its own toys.
- Good puppy management includes ensuring that all of your precious things are out of reach.

Family members

It is important that all adult members of the family follow the same steps when it comes to the education of the puppy. Communication between all members of the family is vitally important to ensure that your puppy receives consistent education.

Everyone needs to understand that anything they do when interacting with the puppy will impact on its future behaviour. This includes playing silly games such as thrusting your hands at the puppy's mouth, allowing the puppy to jump all over you or chasing the puppy. These types of games might be fun at first, but will only serve to turn the puppy into a neurotic, uncontrollable creature.

Children

You will need to be extra diligent if you have young children. Children have a way of exciting a puppy to a degree where much of your good educational work will go out the window. The activities of puppies and children must always be monitored.

The best method is to only allow the puppy and children together when you are able to monitor their actions. Children should be taught to interact with the puppy in a sensible way. Do not allow any silly games where the puppy is pulled and tugged or where hands are used to incite play and biting.

These types of games will only lead to big problems in the future, whereby you will no longer be able to interact with your puppy in a normal way – it will always want to play these silly games that the children taught it.

Other problems may stem from the wrong kind of children's interaction with the puppy. Some children can be too rough, treating the puppy like a toy, and inadvertently hurting it. This can then lead to the puppy's dislike of the child. If this is the case, the puppy will begin to snap at the child to protect itself, which can escalate to a full-on attack if the problem is not rectified quickly.

Visitors

The correct introduction between puppy and visitors is necessary to ensure that future problems don't occur. When visitors come calling, wait for them to settle in, and then bring your puppy in on lead. Do not allow any silly behaviour from either puppy or visitors, as initial impressions are lasting ones. Dogs are creatures of habit and any bad habits formed early on will stay with your puppy forever. An example of the problems that the incorrect interaction with visitors can cause is detailed in the following case history.

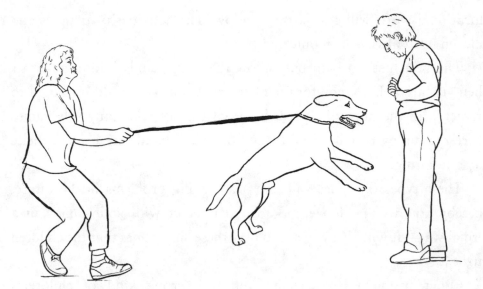

Case history

Mike and Julie's puppy, Cindy, was a very cute and cuddly female shih tzu/ Maltese cross. Until her first encounter with visitors, Cindy was a very well-adjusted and obedient puppy. Problems began when Mike's younger brother David came to visit one day.

David became very excited when he first met Cindy and began roughing her up and playing chasing games with her, which lasted for some time. During the games Cindy became very excited and when utterly exhausted, she began to snap and growl. David continued the games. Although Mike and Julie were a little concerned at the time, they could see no reason for stopping the games as Cindy seemed to be having a lot of fun.

However, whenever David or any other visitor arrived, Cindy would become very excited and completely out of control. She'd begin by barking to be let in and would then bark and jump all over the visitors, until no one could hear themselves think. The more Mike and Julie tried to stop her, the more excited and out-of-control she became.

They finally called in Bark Busters™. Firstly we explained that Mike and Julie had gone wrong by allowing visitors to their house to interact with Cindy in such a way that she now expected all visitors to play crazy games with her.

David's behaviour had created a bad and lasting impression on Cindy and one that was going to spell Cindy's demise if it couldn't be reversed quickly. Mike and Julie had begun to receive complaints from the neighbours about Cindy's barking.

We explained that the behaviour could be reversed, but it would take due diligence from them and complete control of visitor's behaviour in the future. They agreed that Cindy was worth the effort.

The first step was to teach them how to be the leader of the pack. Cindy could not be let in when she was barking, and when visitors did arrive, she must be put on lead. Cindy had to be taught to be calm. Under no circumstances were the visitors allowed to play with her.

To begin with no visitors were permitted to pat Cindy. Instead they were asked to sit down and remain very calm, completely ignoring her. The rationale for this was to teach Cindy that visitors were boring so that she would lose interest in them. This was tough love as Cindy was the most adorable little dog you could imagine. However, it was a necessary step to erase the memory of that excitement rush she had experienced when she first encountered a visitor and to replace it with the thought that visitors are calm creatures and not much fun.

Cindy's behaviour improved each time visitors arrived. Now she waits patiently at the door until Mike or Julie let her in. Then she goes and sniffs the visitors with a happy, wagging tail and lies down nearby.

Mike and Julie will eventually be able to allow visitors to pat Cindy once she has sniffed them, but under no circumstances will they be allowed to play boisterous games with her.

Lead training

The introduction of your puppy to the lead must be done in a very gentle, patient way. Firstly, fit a soft leather or webbing collar (such as the Bark Busters™ Training Collar), ensuring that you can slip two fingers under the collar with ease. Be sure to use this two-finger method weekly to check the fit of the collar as puppies grow quickly. Allow five days for your puppy to become accustomed to its new collar before commencing lead training.

The lead is an alien concept to a dog and especially an impressionable young pup. Incorrect introduction to the lead may cause severe trauma.

The safest way to introduce the lead is at feed times. Your puppy's focus at feed times will be on food, therefore distracting it from the lead.

If the lead appears every time the food does, then positive experiences of the lead will occur in the pup's mind. Allow a further five days of feeding and fitting the lead during meal times, then on the sixth day pick up the lead and allow your puppy to lead you where it wants to go. At this stage do not offer any resistance.

Continue with this method for three days, and then start to take control. Stop in your tracks, facing your puppy, and crouch down to wait for your puppy to approach you. Then give praise and back away, repeating the crouching and praising.

At first your puppy might put up some resistance, because it enjoyed leading you and won't understand what is now required. It's a new concept, so be patient and use lots of encouragement.

Once your puppy is coming to you reliably each time you stop, then the next time you stop, instead of facing your puppy, turn your back.

Crouch, looking over your shoulder, and encourage your puppy to come up on your left side, praising it when it does.

Now you will need to take some steps, remaining in the crouched position. Edge forward, encouraging your dog to take the steps itself without you having to force it.

Continue this for the next two days or until you can stand up facing the way you are going, with your puppy walking happily on your left side.

Equipment
- Soft fitting leather or webbing collar or Bark Busters™ training collar
- Soft 6 ft (1.8 metre) cotton-webbing lead

Going for walks

Puppies should not be walked until they have had their final immunisation injection, which varies according to the views of different veterinarians, but is generally not until they are at least 16 weeks of age.

Lead training of your puppy can commence earlier as described above and should be carried out in the puppy's yard.

When your puppy is old enough to take for walks, start by only taking it on short walks no further than to the end of the street or a few blocks away.

Sit near bus stops or train stations, accustoming your puppy to all of the associated sounds. Some puppies might want to flee, and run home, but don't allow this. Insist that they cope with the sounds, sitting there until they calm down.

If you encounter aggressive dogs behind fences, that bark and carry on when you and your puppy walk past, cross to the other side of the

street and walk your puppy up and down several times. Your puppy must learn that these dogs cannot harm them.

If you meet other people walking their dogs while out on your walk, don't allow the dogs to interact. Keep your distance. Some older dogs have been known to snap at or attack puppies, leaving their victims traumatised for any future walks.

Your puppy must learn to tolerate other dogs, but it is not absolutely necessary for them to fraternise. In the dog world, puppies have no pack status. They are lowly subordinates, so mature dogs will dish out disciplinary action at the drop of a hat. This disciplinary action by older dogs outside of their pack can leave puppies traumatised to such a degree that they may either become aggressive to all dogs they meet in the street or refuse to go anywhere near other dogs they meet while out walking.

The plight of the dog in the next case history clearly shows how normal puppies that have been attacked in this way can become traumatised to the point where they pose a danger to other dogs.

Case history

Bruno, a Rhodesian ridgeback, was the apple of his owner Michael's eye. Playful and outgoing, he loved everyone.

Bruno would greet every dog he met, jumping all over them with joy, until one day when he did this to the wrong dog. A large crossbred dog attacked Bruno, knocking him to the ground. Bruno panicked, and immediately ran from the park and headed for home, narrowly missing two passing cars.

From that day on, Bruno was a different puppy, who did not want to go for his walk. He would shiver and shake each time Michael brought out the lead.

Michael would have to drag him to the park, where Bruno would stay close to Michael, refusing to leave his side. He began to growl each time a dog came near, curling his lip up at each dog that approached to have a sniff of him.

As Bruno began to grow and mature, Michael became concerned. He had long since stopped taking him to the leash-free park. Instead he started taking him out only at night.

Then one evening while out walking in a local park, he saw a man with a dog enter the park, letting the dog off the lead. It bounded towards Bruno and Michael. Michael yelled at the man to call his dog back, but the man called back, saying that there was no problem as his dog wasn't aggressive.

Michael had no time to respond before Bruno grabbed the dog by the throat, cutting off the dog's air. Michael and the man tried in vain to get Bruno to release his grip, however the dog died.

Michael had Bruno put to sleep the next day.

Stories like this one clearly show how a beautiful, fun-loving puppy can be turned into a determined killer. Puppies must be protected when around adult dogs to prevent an attack such as the one that happened to Bruno.

Examination

You should be able to do an examination of your puppy without too much fuss. Place your puppy on lead and begin by checking the ears, the mouth, lifting the paws and checking under the tail. This examination process is important to ensure that your puppy will be a willing participant in any future vet checks.

Grooming

Place your puppy on a lead and lift it onto a stable table. Begin by grooming the neck area using a firm bristle brush, working your way down the body to the tail. If your puppy overreacts, freeze your actions and growl 'Bah'. Wait for your puppy to stop its behaviour, then start brushing again, praising your puppy when it allows you to brush without trying to bite the brush.

Grooming parlours

Once you are able to groom your puppy without problems, you could consider having your puppy groomed professionally.

It is wise to find out about all the grooming parlours in your area prior to booking your puppy in. The right grooming parlour will have good control over their charges without meting out any harsh disciplinary action. They will be very obliging, with no objections to you observing them at work.

Let the grooming parlour proprietor know that your puppy is a novice but that you have been doing some basic grooming at home. Tell them that you would like to stay the first couple of times until your puppy gets to know them.

Correct etiquette

Proper eating etiquette is important. Your puppy should sit and wait while you place its meal on the ground, then wait for the 'pick it up' or 'please eat' command. This exercise should be carried out on lead first. Place your puppy on lead and ask it to sit. Then place the food on the ground in front of it.

If your puppy tries to eat before being commanded, step on the lead and say 'Bah'. Wait for it to sit again, then praise it with 'Good boy'. Wait a few seconds then say 'Free'.

Repeat this exercise daily. Eventually you will be able to do this exercise with your puppy off lead.

Later you can extend this exercise to include situations where food is placed on coffee tables or in children's hands, using the same correction process.

Come when called

All puppies should be trained to 'come when called'. Dogs are not born understanding our language. They must be trained to respond to our requests.

Step 1:

The most effective and efficient way to train your puppy to come when called is to conduct the preliminary training on a long lead.

Allow your puppy to wander off on the lead. In a soft, melodic tone request it to come, for example, 'Fido, come'. Then tug gently on the lead, saying 'Bah'. The verbal correction is used in this case to let your

puppy know that you are displeased with its refusal to respond immediately to your voice command. Guide your puppy to you.

Make a big fuss of your puppy when it approaches, wait a few seconds, then let it wander off again. This exercise should be practised daily.

Step 2:

When your puppy is coming each time you gently tug, your next step is to work towards having your puppy come when called without the lead.

Begin by only using the lead as a 'safety net', a precaution in case your puppy refuses your requests.

Now see if your puppy will come to you without the tug.

Do not remove the lead until your dog is reliably coming each time you call. Puppies that prove to be more difficult should be left on lead a little longer until they are responding to your voice commands alone.

Puppy school

These days it is very acceptable for puppies to attend 'puppy school' or education classes for young puppies. Check the Yellow Pages for venues or contact your local Bark Busters™ representative (see page 228).

The first important step in your search for a puppy school is to find out the school's procedure for training puppies, as methods differ from one school to another. Ensure that the school you choose does not use 'Alpha rolling', any form of 'scruffing' or 'free-for-alls'.

Alpha rolling

Alpha rolling is a widely used training technique, where puppies are rolled onto their backs as a way of gaining control. This technique should *never* be used on any puppy or dog as it can cause aggression towards owners as well as a dislike for hands.

Scruffing

Scruffing is another commonly used technique for disciplining naughty puppies. The mischievous pup is grabbed by the scruff of the neck and shaken, which causes a dislike for the hands. It is *never* necessary to use physical force to control a puppy.

Free-for-alls

This term is used to describe a practice where puppies of different sizes and varying personality types are allowed off the lead to play at puppy school and romp together. This practice creates future dog aggression problems, with some puppies becoming aggressive towards all dogs.

The reason why 'free-for-alls' result in aggression problems as puppies grow is that other puppies were allowed to dominate them during the 'free-for-all' periods permitted at some puppy schools. The puppies consequently believe that they either dominate other dogs or are dominated themselves.

It is totally unnecessary for puppies to be socialised in this fashion. They should only ever be socialised on lead, where no domination by other puppies can occur.

Pool safety

If you have a pool, you will definitely need to teach your puppy some pool safety strategies. Dogs are normally very good swimmers but instinctively will try to exit a pool where they went in. This instinct stems from the fact that when their wild ancestors fell into icy waters, they needed to exit quickly to avoid hypothermia and would instinctively climb out at the exact spot they fell in. This makes a lot of sense in the wild, but very little sense in suburbia where a backyard pool has smooth edges, providing no grip for a dog to exit the way it fell in.

Special training is required to teach the puppy where to exit. A dog or puppy must be shown how to find the stairs or a suitable exit, if it does accidentally fall in. Many people mistakenly believe that their dog is safe around pools based on the fact that it never goes near the edge or is frightened of the water. This is a dangerous assumption because puppies have been known to drown in backyard pools, after their owners had previously seen them shy away from the water.

Remember that puppies are like young children, easily distracted, and can fall into a pool while playing, chasing a butterfly or just trying to get a drink. Therefore pool safety is of paramount importance to your puppy's welfare, regardless of whether or not it appears to like the water.

Step 1:

Establish where your puppy or dog can easily exit the water. If there is no easy exit, create one by installing either a rubber grip mat or a landing platform that hangs into the pool that would allow your puppy or dog to raise itself above the water.

Then attach a long, lightweight lead, and lower or drop your puppy or dog into the pool at the furthest point from the exit. Using the lead, gradually direct the puppy to the exit steps. Ensure that it can exit unaided.

Some dogs really panic when dropped into the water. Keep your wits about you if this happens. Use the lead to direct your puppy to safety. Be careful not to get your puppy tangled in the lead as this could cause complications with its ability to swim.

Step 2:

Continue with several more practices, showing your charge where to exit. Now see if your dog can exit without your help. Still holding on to the lead for emergencies, see if he can swim unaided to the exit spot.

Once your puppy is exiting by himself, he should be ready for step three. Be careful not to exhaust a little puppy. These steps might have to be done over a period of a few days to ensure that it does not become overtired.

Step 3:

Providing your puppy has shown that it is a capable swimmer or you are ready to scoop him to safety, you can now try a solo swim.

Place your puppy in the water off lead, ensuring that it is swimming without any difficulty. Now let it make its own way. Do not call your puppy or stand near the exit spot. It must learn to find the way out by itself. Remember that you might not be there the day it accidentally falls in, so it must be able to save itself. However, be ready and prepared to dive in if your puppy gets into difficulties.

Warning

Do not attempt any of the pool safety steps if you are not a competent, capable swimmer.

Summary:

- Dogs in the wild receive their education from the pack, so you must be your dog's educator.
- Dogs need to feel secure in the knowledge that they have a strong leader.
- Practice good puppy management with both inside and outside-housed puppies.
- Ensure that all members of the family participate in the puppy's education and that everyones' methods are consistent with those of other family members.
- All training of puppies must be delivered gently. Never discipline your puppy physically.
- Pool safety training is imperative if you have a backyard swimming pool.

5

Common health problems

A well-bred, stress-free, happy, and well-nurtured puppy should experience very few health problems. However, if your puppy has had a bad start in life, is the runt of the litter or is easily stressed, it may be prone to health problems at some period in its life.

The following are common canine health problems.

Hot spots

Hot spots generally occur at the base of the spine near the dog's tail, and are easily recognised. Biting and consequent thinning of the dog's hair leads to the dog's flesh being very visible through the hair. The spot may also be wet where the dog has begun to bite or lick at the itchy skin.

The common causes of hot spots are inactivity, being overfed, or eating too much red meat or protein. Some food colourings or preservatives may also cause a flare-up.

This condition may also be caused by an allergic reaction to a fleabite. When a flea bites a dog it injects a protein via its saliva into the dog's flesh, causing the skin to become inflamed and itchy. The dog then bites the area that it can reach, which usually is at the base of the tail, making the problem worse.

Eliminating red meat or an abundance of protein from the dog's diet and replacing it with chicken can sometimes be helpful because it assists in cooling the dog's system. Where fleas are a problem, the use of a flea repellent is recommended. If the problem is detected early when the skin is still unbroken, a product known as Bitter Apple can be used to deter the dog from biting. Bitter Apple is available from pet stores, your local Bark Busters™ office, or by visiting our website (see page 228).

If problems persist, call your local vet for advice.

First aid:

- Have someone assist you by holding your dog.
- Cut hair away from the infected area.
- Wash the area with a diluted solution of antiseptic, and blot it dry with a clean towel.
- Apply cortisone or antibacterial cream.
- Contact your vet if problems persist.

Eczema

Like human eczema, eczema in dogs is caused by allergies. Dogs can have allergies to food, certain grasses, sprays and fleas. Isolating the exact cause of a dog's eczema sometimes proves difficult. Some dogs suffer from what is known as 'flea allergy'. The best cure for this is to keep the dog completely flea free, which is more difficult than it sounds. Some dogs will flare up after just one fleabite. Most cases of canine eczema disappear once the flea problem is addressed.

There are some very good flea prevention treatments on the market. Consult your vet for the best treatment for your dog.

Kennel cough

As the name suggests, this is a highly contagious airborne viral disease that spreads through boarding kennels. Before being accepted for boarding at a kennel, dogs must be immunised against both strains of the virus. Dogs are generally immunised against this in the course of their normal injections.

Kennel cough does not only occur in boarding kennels, although cases of dogs isolated to the backyard contracting the disease are generally rare. Dogs suffering stress are more prone to catching kennel cough than other dogs.

Symptoms include a very dry, hacking cough, which may result in the dog coughing up mucus, and a runny nose.

Mites

As a rule, healthy dogs do not suffer from mites. Signs that a dog has mites include vigorous scratching of the ears, or moaning and whining. The dog may also constantly shake its head or hold its head slightly on one side. If your dog has any of these symptoms, the vet will be able to diagnose the problem and prescribe eardrops to treat the problem quickly.

Constipation

It's a good idea to pick up your dog's droppings on a daily basis so that you can spot any irregularities in your dog's bowel movements. Depending on its diet, a dog will have at least one bowel movement per day. If your dog repeatedly tries to pass a bowel movement without success, is straining, listless or has a decreased appetite, it may be suffering from constipation, which may be caused by it being fed too many bones in the heat of the day. Never feed your dog cooked bones, as they are another cause of constipation. A cooked bone can splinter, and sometimes lodge in the dog's intestines.

Raw bones are the canine's natural toothbrush and are highly beneficial to the dog's wellbeing, provided they are not fed in the heat of the day.

Adding flaxseed or cod liver oil to the dog's diet may cure constipation. Consult a vet if the problem persists.

Diarrhoea

The causes of diarrhoea are numerous, ranging from stress, diet changes, and parasites to intestinal diseases. Diarrhoea may be an early warning sign of serious illness.

Any puppy with diarrhoea should be taken to the vet immediately, especially if there has been no recent change of diet. Young puppies are very susceptible to disease, so it is better to be safe than sorry.

Milk can sometimes cause diarrhoea, so it is best to give your puppy 'puppy milk', which is available from vets and pet shops.

Canine distemper

Due to modern immunisation, distemper is virtually unheard of nowadays. However, it may still pose a threat to puppies, particularly when they are being re-housed. The first sign of canine distemper is fever, which may be difficult to detect, as your dog will simply appear to be slightly lethargic for a few days.

A dry nose is one obvious symptom of the disease, but it does not necessarily mean your dog has canine distemper.

Some dogs will lose the power in their back legs or their legs may become wobbly if they are suffering from canine distemper (this can also be a sign of the start of tick paralysis).

Symptoms of advanced canine distemper include shaking and hallucinations, the dog not recognising people they are familiar with or the dog attacking the air around them or their owner.

The canine distemper virus attacks the dog's brain, causing a form of 'canine madness'. It does not always prove fatal, however, if it is not treated early, the chances of recovery are very slim.

Dogs receive natural immunity to canine distemper from their mother's milk. Puppies are now also immunised against the disease between the ages of six and eight weeks.

Canine hepatitis

Like human hepatitis, canine hepatitis is a virus that attacks the liver. Any dog that is regularly boarded or travels frequently should be immunised against hepatitis.

Symptoms of canine hepatitis include nausea, appearance of jaundice, depression and vomiting.

Canine Leptospirosis

The symptoms of canine leptospirosis may be mistaken for hepatitis. Ensure that your dog is properly diagnosed as this disease can be passed on to humans. Seek veterinary attention immediately.

Parvo virus

It is not widely known where this disease originated. It appears to be a strain of canine distemper that developed during the mid-1970s. Parvovirus kills its host very rapidly. I have seen otherwise healthy adult dogs succumb to it very quickly. Adult dogs are at greater risk when they are going through a stressful period, such as when being re-housed or being boarded.

Symptoms include depression and severe diarrhoea (reddish in colour, with a pungent smell). Seek veterinary advice quickly as intravenous fluids are urgently needed.

A dose of sodium ascorbate (Vitamin C) can act as an effective preventative treatment.

Rabies

Rabies can affect nearly every living creature on earth. This disease attacks the central nervous system, and once contracted, death is inevitable. Rabies has a long incubation period, so it may take many months to surface.

Symptoms of rabies include personality changes, frothing at the mouth, and biting.

There has been no recorded case of rabies in Australia.

6

Dealing with an adolescent dog

A dog's adolescence occurs from six months to 14 months of age. It is around about this time that its body begins to produce sex hormones and it begins to behave erratically.

Dogs age approximately seven years to our one year and they begin to mature once they are full-grown but will not be fully developed until much later. Dogs continue growing until they reach 12 months of age for normal dogs and 24 months for giant breeds, then when the growing ceases, they begin to fill out and mature both mentally and physically. The breeds that generally have longer adolescent periods than others include labradors, great danes, Irish wolfhounds, Newfoundlands, malamutes, German shepherds, Belgian shepherds, dalmatians, old English sheepdogs, airedales and weimaraners.

Dog adolescence is not unlike human adolescence. In the same way that teenagers become more difficult to control as they reach puberty, your adolescent dog will launch challenges to your leadership. A previously well-behaved and obedient puppy can become a mischievous rascal overnight, ignoring everything you say. A large percentage of surrendered dogs are adolescent dogs, with the six to 12 month's age-group the one most often abandoned.

However, if you are well prepared for your dog's adolescence, you will survive without too much stress and heartache. By making preparations early on in your dog's life, you can ensure that you sail through your dog's teenage years trouble free.

Survival tips for the owners of adolescent dogs

Tip 1:

Commence your dog's training long before it reaches adolescence. By the time your dog reaches adolescence, you will already have completed the essential groundwork and established control. Training a puppy from its first, formative months ensures stability in the future.

Tip 2:

Accustom your puppy to a pen from day one so that you have control over your dog's environment. Any destructive behaviour, which may escalate during adolescence, can then be controlled and dramatically reduced. Locking your dog away each time you go out or when you are unable to monitor its behaviour will reduce the amount of chewing and digging it does.

Tip 3:

Be consistent by displaying good leadership and controlling any unwarranted behaviour. A dog that is reaching maturity will be less likely to challenge its owner if it perceives them to be a strong leader. Dogs instinctively challenge the pack leader when they perceive the leader to be losing touch. An adolescent dog is less likely to challenge a strong leader and will breeze through adolescence feeling safe and secure in its environment.

Tip 4:

Make sure your dog is kept busy and entertained. Its day is as long as yours, and with much less activity to fill it, it's not difficult to imagine why they get up to mischief.

Case history

Penny was an exuberant female dalmatian. Her owners, Kylie and Greg, were saving up to buy a larger home, but in the meantime there was limited space in their backyard, with only enough room for the clothesline and Penny's kennel. I was called in to see if I could stop Penny from pulling washing off the line. I explained to Kylie and Greg that the choices of activity for Penny were very limited: the washing line or the kennel.

It was obvious that this dog was bored and in need of stimulation. I prescribed a Buster Cube and a rubber Kong toy for Penny to play with and suggested that the washing line be wound right up and out of Penny's reach. I also recommended that they build her a sandpit and install a small child's wading pool. In no time Penny's yard was a veritable doggy paradise.

It is unreasonable to expect that a dog will be able to just sit for hours on end without any form of mental stimulation and not become destructive. With some strategic playthings to keep them occupied, your dog will enjoy a more pleasurable life and you will sail through your dog's adolescence virtually trouble free.

Unruly behaviour in the house

Good house manners from an adolescent dog include calm behaviour when it enters the house. A dog that bounds through the house, knocking everything flying, jumping on the sofa, and everyone in the house, is not behaving properly.

Put your dog on the lead and allow the lead to trail on the ground. If your dog bounds through the door, step on the lead to restrict your dog's progress. Growl 'Bah'. This will instantly let your dog know that you disapprove of its wild behaviour. Praise your dog when it reacts favourably. Continue this process as your dog moves around the home, stepping on the lead each time it attempts to bound ahead of you or becomes excited. Growl each time, and then praise any calm behaviour.

In the initial stages of this education process you will be growling a lot until your dog learns the type of behaviour you expect. Over the next few days, you will begin to see an improvement. Your dog will begin to stop and check with you before doing anything. This is a good sign that you are beginning to get the message through that you are the boss.

When you are confident that your dog can be controlled by your voice alone, take it off the lead and use your correction word 'Bah' to let your dog know that you are still in control. If your dog returns to its old ways the instant the lead comes off, you have taken the lead off too early. Place the lead back on and persevere a little longer. It can take up to five weeks to change a dog's behaviour permanently.

Food stealing

Dogs have no sense of right or wrong. Food left unattended is an open invitation to any young, uneducated dog. To stop a dog from stealing food, set the scene. Place some food on a kitchen bench or a coffee table, then bring your dog in on lead. Wait for him to move towards the food, then step on the lead and growl 'Bah'. Give praise when your dog responds. Repeat several times until your dog ignores the food altogether.

Jumping on the bed or sofa

Attach a lead and allow it to trail on the ground. Wait for your dog to head towards the bed or sofa, catching it just before it reaches the item of furniture, then step on the lead, growl and praise once your dog reacts favourably. If your dog is too quick for you or it ignores you, then pick up the lead and guide it off the furniture, growling as you do, then praising it when it is on the floor again.

Repeat this several times until your dog ceases to jump on the object. Now try to entice your dog onto the object by sitting or lying on it yourself. Growl if your dog tries to hop on, using the lead to prevent it from doing so. Praise your dog when all four of its feet are on the ground.

Pestering you at the dinner table

At mealtimes it is unwise to feed your dog tidbits from the table as this practice only encourages bad habits. A dog that is never fed from the table in this way never anticipates it happening. Try to feed your dog at

the same time you are eating your meals, then if it returns to pester you after it has eaten, stand up to your full height, growl 'Bah', and point away from the table, indicating you do not want it near the table at this time. Remember to praise your dog the instant it responds, then sit down and finish your meal.

Pulling on the lead

Dogs will automatically pull when they feel something pull against them. They need to be taught that pulling is wrong and will not be tolerated. Some people give up on walking their dog because they cannot get control and their dog just simply pulls them along, leaving them hanging on for dear life.

What people tend to do when this happens is shorten the lead. But this only makes the dog pull more as the short lead provides no leverage and control is completely lost.

At Bark Busters™ we recommend that owners walk their dog on a loose, six-foot (1.8 metre) lead as it provides more leverage. The first thing we do is slow them down. The owners of adolescent dogs are generally accustomed to rushing everywhere they go. The dog cannot be trained to concentrate at this fast pace. They must be slowed down in order to get them to focus on the job at hand. This slow walking method works very effectively.

Because dogs will naturally pull on a lead, they cannot learn to walk correctly if the lead is always tight. It must be loosened and then snapped back to communicate to the dog that pulling is unhelpful. This snap and release process will let the dog know what you expect.

To re-cap, the correct process for walking an adolescent dog is to walk slowly, using a six-foot (1.8 metre) lead and then snapping and releasing. Leather collars, although very popular, are not the most suitable choice of training equipment for dogs. A Bark Busters™ halti or check collar are far better than a normal fixed leather collar.

Summary:

- A dog's adolescence begins at approximately six months of age.
- Maturity in dogs is reached anywhere from twelve months to two years, with some breeds taking up to four years.
- To stave off problems associated with adolescence, it is best to commence your dog's training long before it reaches that stage.
- The building of a pen can save you a lot of heartache from adolescent destructive behaviour.
- Be consistent – adolescent dogs especially need strong leadership.
- Provide lots of entertaining and educational toys.

7

Understanding your dog's behaviour

Dog psychology

Dogs learn by association and from experience. They must experience something to be able to understand it, as it cannot be explained to them. Dogs do not have comprehension in the same way that humans do. They are really creatures of habit as well as of the moment. When something happens that has happened before they will expect that the exact same thing is about to happen again. For example, when its owner opens the fridge and gives a dog a treat, the next time the owner goes to the fridge, the dog might immediately sit in anticipation of another treat.

This is known as learning by association. The dog has learnt to associate the opening of the fridge door with the receiving of food, even though the fridge door might be opened 20 times a day without the dog receiving a treat.

Problem solvers

Some very intelligent dogs will take this a bit further by indicating to their owners that they want a treat by sitting in front of the fridge until they are given one.

Dogs are also very capable of solving problems. They can see something on the other side of a fence and might work out that by digging under the fence, they can reach the object. We can put this down to partly instinct and partly their ability for problem solving.

Some dogs possess a very high level of intelligence and have an innate ability to solve even the most complex of problems. These dogs are higher up the intelligence scale and will outsmart some pretty intelligent owners. An example of the highly intelligent canine that can solve specific problems occurs in the following case history of our bull terrier 'Bullseye'.

Case history

Bullseye came to us as a seven-month-old stray from the pound. From the day he arrived we knew there was something special about him. He seemed almost to have an ability to read our minds and he won our hearts immediately.

As time passed we noticed the intelligence that Bullseye possessed. At the time he was our only dog and he was given a very special sleeping bag to sleep on. Each day he would take the sleeping bag out into the sun, spread it out on the lawn and sun himself.

Then each afternoon he would pick it up in his mouth, putting it back in his kennel. He would spend time spreading it out in the interior of the kennel, pushing it into the corners with his nose. He was so thorough about this that you could imagine that the carpet layers had been to do the job.

This became his daily ritual, until the day two other dogs came into our lives, a doberman named Kaydee, aged 14 months, and a four-year-old airedale named Harry.

We arrived home one day to find that Kaydee and Harry had ripped Bullseye's special sleeping bag into a million pieces. I will never forget the sight of Bullseye sitting on the back patio looking out over the devastation spread out on the lawn, as far as the eye could see. His special sleeping bag was now just a tattered mess.

With our two new dogs, Kaydee and Harry, experiencing the stress of settling into a new home, we decided that trampoline beds in the short term might be a better option. So the following day we bought three trampoline beds.

At first Bullseye wasn't overly impressed, as he could not move his out into the sun, which he had been able to with his sleeping bag. He made several attempts to grab the side of the bed in his mouth and move it, but it was too hard for his mouth. He gave up in disgust.

Then approximately one week later, we could hardly believe our eyes when Bullseye solved the problem. He crawled under the trampoline bed and began to walk it out onto the lawn. He looked like a crab with its shell on its back as he found the right spot, dropped to the ground and crawled out from underneath the trampoline bed, then proceeded to hop on top and sun himself. Bullseye had solved the problem of how to get his bed into the sun.

We witnessed many such wonderful problem-solving situations over the next 13 years. On one occasion we gave Bullseye some pizza in the pizza box on a high veranda. He began eating the pizza and as he did so, the box edged precariously close to the edge of the veranda. Each time it did, Bullseye would grab it in his mouth and pull it back and begin eating again.

Then tiring of this ritual, he picked the box up in his mouth complete with the rest of the pizza and carried it down the stairs to finish his snack in peace on the lawn. This dog was one of the best problem-solving dogs I have ever known.

How dogs learn

Dogs learn by experiencing something which is then locked into their memory.

Pavlov conducted experiments to show the way dogs learn. In one experiment a bell was rung and then the dogs were fed. He conducted this experiment over a period of time. The dogs eventually began to salivate when they heard the bell ring. He could thus deduce from this experiment that dogs learn by association.

Learning by association

The easiest way to demonstrate how dogs learn by association is to put a red hat on every time you feed your dog. If you were to put that hat on at another time, your dog would become very excited, expecting that it would be fed shortly. When it wasn't fed, it would become confused.

Dogs learn to associate that one specific thing or a series of events immediately precedes another. We can observe this daily when we prepare to take our dogs for a walk. We get ready, put on runners, and go to the cupboard where the dogs' leads are kept. The dogs associate the sequence of events as meaning 'we are going for a walk'.

Because of the dog's ability to interpret a sequence of events, and then anticipate a certain thing will eventuate, I avoid establishing routines of either going out alone or walking my dogs. This prevents my dogs from becoming excited until I actually produce the lead. It doesn't matter how many times I go to that particular cupboard, my dogs do not overreact. I have adopted this 'no routine' method for everything I do. For example, some days I take my dogs to work, and other days I don't. This prevents the excitable behaviour associated with certain actions and reduces my dogs' stress levels at those times when the routine might be broken, such as during holidays.

Learning by experience

Learning from experience simply means that the dog has to experience something before it can learn. We can say to a child 'the stove is hot' and they will know what we mean. However, a dog would have to touch it to know it's hot. The dog's memory plays a large role in its ability to learn by experience. A dog has an excellent memory – generally it only needs to experience something once and this memory is locked in for ever.

A dog's amazing memory has its disadvantages as bad experiences are also locked in. A dog that is attacked by another dog as a puppy may have this memory locked in for ever, resulting in a future fear of all other dogs.

At Bark Busters™ we have discovered that these 'locked-in' experiences can be unlocked and reversed through 'behavioural modification', which simply means re-programming the dog to have some good experiences with other dogs. This re-programming takes approximately five weeks of regularly positive exposure to other dogs.

Telling time

A dog's ability to judge time is also part of its ability to learn by association. I believe they associate other events that occur just prior to an event such as their owner arriving home, for example, the afternoon shadows cast on the walls of the house by the sun. Other associations with time might include such things as the next-door neighbour's children arriving home from school, or the man in the street who arrives home on his motorbike five minutes before the dog's owner arrives home.

Dogs associate what is happening at that time or just prior to the event. My dogs will watch me go to the sink several times a day without showing any real interest. Yet when I go to the sink near their dinnertime they become very interested in what I'm doing. They evidently have a way of judging the time, knowing that the time for their dinner is near.

Can dogs distinguish right from wrong?

Dogs have no concept of right or wrong. When a dog does something, its actions are based on instinct. A dog will explore and investigate everything in much the same way that children do. When a dog experiences something pleasurable, it will more than likely return over and over again to that source of entertainment.

An example of this could be a dog that chases the garden hose while its owner is watering the garden. The exhilarating pleasure experienced by the dog will incite it to return to that type of activity over and over again. However, if the dog was to have an unpleasant experience while chasing the hose, it's likely that it would try to avoid the hose next time.

Dogs are not very interested in continuing to do that which gives them no pleasure. The right deterrent can very quickly make a dog cease its bad behaviour. Never try to punish the dog using the hose or by squirting the hose at your dog. This would only incite the dog to chase it with more vigour.

In situations like the one described above, a dog needs the guidance and direction of its pack leader. Dogs will not go against the will of a strong leader. The concept of right or wrong does not enter the dog's mind – it takes its lead from what the pack leader will or won't allow.

There are specific behavioural problems that can be solved by working out a way to make it appear as if the object that your dog is chewing, is 'correcting' your dog. This might sound silly but it basically means making the object seem responsible for the dog's bad experience.

Imagine your dog is chewing an inanimate object such as a shoe. You could spray a harmless deterrent onto the shoe, which would give the dog the bad experience. The dog would then think that the object has delivered the unpleasant experience. The dog wouldn't think, 'It was my owner who sprayed that on the shoe'. The dog isn't learning right from wrong. It is simply learning what gives it pleasure and what causes it discomfort.

The effect of adrenaline

This type of deterrent would not work where the dog is attacking something such as a lawn mower or an animate object, such as the garden hose. The movement of animate objects excites the dog, releasing adrenaline into the blood stream, which overrides any discomfort the dog might be feeling. The dog views moving objects as creatures that are alive and it deals with them in the only way it understands.

Adrenaline affects the dog's ability to learn. The only thing that overrides the surge of adrenaline in the blood in these situations is if the pack leader (the owner) shows the dog that its behaviour is unacceptable. The dog learns to behave in that way when the pack leader is present.

The dog might persist with the bad behaviour when the pack leader isn't present as the dog has learned by association that the behaviour won't be tolerated when the pack leader is around.

In some cases the correction mechanism ('Bah' and clap) required for stopping the undesirable behaviour will need to be delivered at other times when the adrenaline is not present. Once your dog has learned to recognise the correction process, it will then respond at those times when adrenaline is present.

Summary:

- Dogs learn in two ways – by association and experience.
- Dogs do not know right from wrong. They learn this from us.
- Adrenaline affects your dog's learning ability.

8

Identifying your dog's temperament

It is possible to determine a dog's temperament and judge its confidence very quickly by observing how it reacts when you first meet it. Most dogs will immediately test the waters because they want to see if they can dominate you. Dogs act in this way when they first meet another dog. They approach each other displaying certain body language to determine which dog is the most dominant.

A dog's parents and ancestors determine its temperament. Traces of the personalities of its mother and father will be found in each puppy, with some strains of a particular parent sometimes stronger in individual puppies. To determine the type of personality your dog will have, observe its parents.

The temperament and confidence of each individual dog determines how they react to each other. Confident dogs will stiffen as the other dog approaches. When confronted with this type of stance, a less dominant dog will lower its height and dart about in front of the more dominant dog.

This lowering and darting tells the other dog that it poses no threat. It also means that the subordinate dog is reading loud and clear that the more dominant dog could attack at any second, and is doing all in its power to appease the dominator.

When two dogs of equally dominant temperament meet on neutral territory, they will approach each other, mirroring the other dog's stance. They will then usually both walk around each other stiff legged, sizing each other up, which will either result in the dogs fighting or just tentatively moving off in their own direction without any altercation.

However, if the same two dogs meet in a leash-free park where over a period of time they have established a pecking order with the other dogs that regularly attend, the interaction between the two dominant dogs might be different. More than likely they will play, depending on whether or not they have previously determined a pecking order or if their owners are strong leaders. Dominant dogs that have strong leaders or have established pecking orders with the park hierarchy are more likely to play, to determine the strength of their opponent without inflicting injury. A dog with a strong leader will be mindful of the fact that the pack leader makes the decision to fight, not them. They will have one eye on their owner the whole time.

Dogs that have formed into packs, although temporarily, do not want to injure a member of their pack, as they instinctively know that they rely on the rest of the pack for survival.

I believe that the mirroring body language that dogs of similar dominance perform when they first meet is very much like the behaviour of humans when they are trying to establish rapport. Human behaviourists have noted that people who want to be liked by other people will mirror their body language.

Dominant dogs instinctively know the other's strength and want to try everything they can to stave off an attack. Although canines and humans are different in so many ways, I have discovered that in certain respects there are similarities between the two species. Dominant dogs endeavour to gain rapport in an effort to achieve 'A Mexican stand-off'.

Predetermined temperament

A dog's temperament is established from birth. Effective training will improve certain traits, of course, but you cannot change a dog's basic temperament – it's the blueprint with which each puppy is born. Having observed hundreds of puppies over the years, I can always spot the nervous, the timid, the dominant and the middle pack order types, even from a very early age.

Dogs display everything through their body language. If they are the confident type, they will stand as tall as they can. They will push their way to the front, challenging others front on. If they are less confident and unsure of themselves, they will lower their height, move out of the way of others and generally be compliant.

Dogs also use this system to assess humans. In the dogs' mind there is absolutely no difference between dogs and humans. First they will sniff the human to identify who they are. Because of the limitations of their sight, which is binocular, allowing them to spot prey off in the distance but limited when viewing close objects, dogs rely heavily on their sense of smell to identify others.

They immediately attempt to establish the dominance and pecking order of each particular person or dog they meet. Dominance is established by the way that people or dogs react to the dog's advances. The dog will try several things to ascertain how high up the pecking order the human or dog is. This may include jumping on them to see if they will back away, and blocking them with their body to see if they will move around them. They might also move away, enticing the human or dog to follow.

The dog views any kind of submissive behaviour as a sign of a subordinate dog. Subordinate behaviour includes moving around the dog when it blocks your way, stepping back, or overreacting when the dog jumps on you, and following the dog rather than leading. All of this behaviour indicates to the dog that it is higher up the pack order than you are.

The temperament of each dog determines how easy it will be to train. The dominant, higher pack order dogs are more difficult to train. You will only prevail with this type if you assert *your* dominance. The less dominant, lower pack order dogs will be easier to train as you won't need to be too dominant to succeed.

Let us look more closely at the different types of personalities to determine the temperament of your dog.

Lower pack order, more compliant

Dogs with compliant temperaments are very focused on their owners. They will nearly always maintain eye contact whenever their owners are present. They will generally not stray too far, but if they do wander off, they will always keep one eye on their owner.

One command or correction is generally all that is needed with this temperament type. They are generally friendly with most dogs, not wanting to rock the boat.

Higher pack order, less compliant

A less compliant dog will test you. It will stand in your way when you move from room to room, defying your requests to move. It will ignore your commands, and will generally refuse to look at you, and unless you have something it wants, it will prefer to sniff and focus elsewhere. It will rush through doorways in front of you, knocking you out of the way. It will jump on you with great force, almost knocking you to the ground, and will bite your hand if you try to restrain it.

In every litter there are pack leader dogs. This is nature's way of ensuring that each pack has a ready supply of leaders. In the wild, every dog must be eventually capable of leading the pack in case something happens

to the pack leader or several other members of the pack. The order just moves up a notch if something happens to the leader and the next in line in dominance takes up the position. Contrary to popular belief, female dogs are the ones most likely to lead a pack, rather than the alpha male.

Middle pack order, compliant

A middle pack order dog will be a delight to own if you are consistent and its bad habits are addressed early. Any bad habits of this temperament type will generally be due to its owner's inconsistencies. Middle pack order dogs are generally identifiable by their easy-going, non-aggressive, compliant manner. They are dogs that rarely fight other dogs unless really pushed. If they do have any behavioural problems they generally stem from poor leadership.

The middle pack order temperament dogs are very easily trained. However, at Bark Busters™ we are called in to treat many middle pack

order dogs each day and this is largely due to the fact that their owners tend to baby them, leading the dog to believe they have to challenge for leadership. The owners in nearly all of these cases mistakenly think that they have a dominant, stubborn dog on their hands when in fact they have a dog that is happy to be in its place but just needs a consistent leader.

Summary:

- Dogs are individuals, possessing differing personalities.
- Dogs have a predetermined personality at birth.
- Dogs live by pack hierarchy, naturally working out the pecking order.

9

Dealing with common behavioural problems

Many people mistakenly believe that their dog will automatically behave well without any need for formal education. All dogs need education and discipline in order for them to develop into well-adjusted pets. They will develop behavioural problems if this need for discipline is not met.

Most problematic behaviour in dogs occurs because people don't understand the way a dog's mind works. Dogs read body language.

Dogs that feel that they don't have a strong leader will seek one out. I have seen hundreds of cases of dogs digging their way out of their yard to go off and live with the people up the road. Dogs need a strong pack to ensure their survival, so they will join one if they don't have one at home.

A weak, indecisive owner will make their dog feel fearful and vulnerable.

Rushing through gates or doors

If you want to demonstrate to your dog that you are the boss as well as address other behavioural problems, then gate and door training is where you should start to modify your dog's behaviour.

The dog that moves ahead of the pack or is the first through a gate or door is perceived to be the dominant dog. When opening or entering doors or moving from room to room, ensure that you are the first one through all doors. If your dog tries to enter first let it know that it has made a mistake. Growl the 'Bah' word while you simultaneously clap your hands. Stop in your tracks, wait for your dog to stop or move behind you, then praise it. Some more determined dogs might need you to attach a lead at first to ensure that your requests are heeded.

Practise this door training technique regularly. Make sure that you don't get into a situation where you are wrestling with your dog to prevent it beating you through doors. You must always be in control. As time progresses, you can attach a lead and allow it to drag on the ground, stepping on it if your dog rushes through the door or runs ahead of you.

Summary:
- Attach a lead, allowing it to trail.
- Establish leadership by leading the way through all doors.
- Growl 'Bah' and step on the lead to correct the dog's undesirable behaviour.
- Don't get into a wrestling match – make sure you are always in control.

Jumping up

Jumping up is generally a dog's way of testing for dominance. It is also used as a way of asserting dominance. Dogs will instinctively aim for height as height also denotes dominance. Other reasons for jumping up can include being allowed to jump from puppyhood. Puppies are sometimes encouraged to jump by their owners because of their diminutive size, which poses no problems until the dog reaches adulthood.

During puppyhood jumping can be instinctive. In the wild, when a mother dog returned from hunting, she would regurgitate food for her puppies. A puppy jumping up mimics the way puppies would behave in the wild when the mother dog returned to her pups.

Some dog owners believe that their dog is just trying to be friendly, which makes it difficult for them to contemplate correcting their dog's

behaviour. However, the dog is learning to dominate them. All dogs should be trained not to jump.

Whatever the reason for your dog jumping up, the way to solve the problem is by establishing pack leadership. You must show your dog that you are the pack leader and will not tolerate a subordinate dog jumping on you.

To achieve this, behave the way a dominant dog would behave, that is, stand totally still and erect, to your full height. Wait for your dog to jump, timing your correction to coincide with its front feet lifting off the ground. Do not wait until it has landed on you. Growl the correction word 'Bah', clapping your hands loudly at the same time. This behaviour precisely mimics the way a dominant dog would behave when confronted by another dog that was attempting to jump on it. The dominant dog would freeze, stand tall and rigid, and growl or snap at the offender.

This technique will work if your dog has gained respect through other aspects of your training. However, if your dog does not perceive you to be its pack leader, then you will have to use incentives. Be sure to give praise as soon as your dog reacts favourably.

Incentives

Incentives are tools that assist you to get your dog to respond to your voice control. They are not designed for permanent use, just as a method to be phased out once your dog learns to respond to your voice alone. The aim is to use the incentive in conjunction with the voice correction ('Bah'), then after two weeks, use only the voice correction. The incentive can be reintroduced at any time when the voice correction is ignored by your dog.

Water squirter

These are available from most hardware stores or supermarkets, and can be used to spray your dog when it refuses to respond to other methods. Squirt the dog the instant its feet leave the ground, growling the correction word 'Bah' as it does. Praise your dog when it responds favourably, growling and squirting the water the instant it tries to jump again.

Bark Busters™ training pillows

A little pillow-shaped object that emits a high-pitched sound when dropped can also be a useful tool to add force to your correction technique with those dogs that resist the normal methods. These pillows are available through your nearest Bark Busters™ office, with a lesson about how to use them effectively. The idea of the pillow is to break the dog's focus, encouraging it to then place all four feet on the ground. Once this happens you will have an opportunity to praise your dog. Your dog will then know that this is the most desirable position for it to adopt.

Summary:
- By jumping up, your dog is not being friendly, but is trying to dominate.
- Freeze your actions.
- Correct your dog with the 'Bah' word while you clap loudly the instant it lifts its paws off the ground. Don't wait for it to land on you.
- Use a water squirter or Bark Busters™ training pillow as an incentive to change the dog's focus until your dog learns to respond to your voice alone.

Ankle and hand biting

Most dog owners perceive ankle and hand biting as their puppy being playful and believe that the puppy will eventually outgrow this behaviour. Although most dogs do outgrow this behaviour, waiting for them to do so can be painfully slow. Once again, this is a dog's way of testing the waters to see what it can get away with, checking whether its owner is pack leadership material.

To correct this behaviour, freeze your actions, stop in your tracks, and growl the correction word while you loudly clap your hands. Do not move off until your puppy responds. Remember to use the water squirter or the Bark Busters™ training pillow to alter your puppy's focus, if necessary.

Summary:
- Freeze your actions and stop in your tracks.
- Growl the correction word 'Bah' as you clap loudly.
- Use a water squirter or Bark Busters™ training pillow if your dog refuses to respond.

Separation anxiety

Separation anxiety simply means the fear of being left alone. This problem has several causes, one being the incorrect conditioning by the owners, where puppies are over-indulged, and never given the chance to become accustomed to being left alone. Over-indulging your puppy also includes allowing it into the house the moment it cries to be let in or immediately after you arrive home. These actions create separation problems.

Once again the main reason for this behaviour is a lack of strong leadership. Dogs will become very demanding if they feel that they don't have a strong leader. All demands by your dog, such as whimpering, scratching at the back door or barking to be let in must be corrected. Your dog needs to know that you will not tolerate this behaviour. Use your system of correction as previously explained: the 'Bah' word growled while clapping your hands, or use a Bark Busters™ training pillow to alter the dog's focus.

If your dog is outside and you are inside when the demands begin, do not go outside, but correct from inside in the specified way. Your dog must not think that its demands have brought it favourable results, such as you opening the door or letting it inside.

If you are outside and about to leave when your dog begins its demands, use your water squirter, growl the 'Bah' word, and persist until it ceases its demands and moves away.

Bark Busters™ training pillows can be used on the more persistent demand makers. The pillow should be dropped near the dog or aimed near the gate, growling 'Bah' as it lands.

Step 1:

When you arrive home, leave your dog outside rather than going straight to the door to allow it inside the house. You need to monitor your dog's behaviour to see if it will begin to demand to be let in. Then correct it if it does.

Once you are convinced that your dog understands that you won't pander to its demands and is quiet, open the door and allow it in, giving praise. Your dog should be able to remain outside while you are home without any demands being made. Ensure you wait at least 20 minutes. Vary the amount of time you leave your dog waiting, sometimes leaving it up to an hour before you let it inside.

Step 2:

Set up a situation where it appears to your dog that you are going out for the day. Leave the house, then drive the car down the street and sneak back. You must catch your dog making its demands for your return, but do not move into sight. Wait for your dog to begin its actions, for example, barking, scratching or whimpering, then correct the behaviour using the 'Bah' correction word, clap or Bark Busters™ training pillow (available from your nearest Bark Busters™ office, with a lesson).

Step 3:

While home, lock your dog in the laundry or bathroom, and wait quietly near the door for it to start its demands. Correct the behaviour by firstly banging on the door and growling the 'Bah' word. The use of a Bark Busters™ training pillow (available from your nearest Bark Busters™ office, with a lesson) dropped at the base of the door will usually stop the demands of a more difficult dog. Once your dog responds, wait silently for five minutes then let him out. This might seem like tough love, but separation periods where your dog cannot see you are vitally important to affect a cure.

Summary:

- Do not allow your dog into the house as soon as you arrive home.
- Practise setting up situations where you pretend to go out.
- Practise locking your dog away from you and out of sight when you are home.
- Do not respond to any demands the dog makes by rewarding it with your presence. Instead correct the behaviour using the correction process: growl 'Bah' and clap your hands, or use a Bark Busters™ training pillow (available from your nearest Bark Busters™ office, with a lesson).

Fence jumping

Jumping the fence can be a form of separation anxiety. If your dog is escaping when you go out, then more than likely it is a form of separation anxiety. However, if your dog is attempting to jump the fence when you are home, this is generally a sign of a lack of leadership on your behalf.

Dogs that are desperate to escape no matter whether their owners are home or not are feeling vulnerable. They are escaping to join a stronger pack. First you will need to build a secure pen or modify the fence to ensure your dog cannot escape. A plumber's pipe loosely attached to the top of the fence will generally thwart any escape plans. The pipe will spin when the dog jumps up, preventing it from gaining a foothold.

You will need to commence training with your dog because it needs you to establish that you are a strong leader. Obedience training is one way of establishing that it is part of a strong pack and its survival is ensured.

Summary:

- Dogs that escape usually need strong leadership.
- Modify the fence by placing plumber's pipe along the top, or build a secure run.
- Commence obedience training.

Pulling washing off the line

Problems with your dog pulling the washing off the line are best solved by winding the washing up out of the dog's reach or by building a fence to restrict the dog's access to the line.

If correct puppy education is started early on, most puppies can be trained to stay away from the washing line. Each time you hang your

washing out, take your dog with you. Wait for it to take an interest in the washing, then growl 'Bah', praising your dog when it reacts.

A product known as Bitter Apple is a safe and non-toxic method of deterrence that works on a large percentage of dogs. You simply give your dog a taste of the Bitter Apple, then spray it on four old towels and hang them on the four corners of the line. Leave them there for 24 hours, replenishing the spray after that time. Leave the towels another 24 hours. Do not hang any of your clothes on the line during the 48-hour period.

After 48 hours, you should be able to hang your clothes out, but ensure that you leave the towels in place, replenishing the spray each alternate day when you are not hanging out any washing.

Summary:

- Wind your washing way up out of your puppy's reach.
- Educate your puppy while you are hanging the washing out.
- Bitter Apple can be used for persistent problems with puppies and washing on the line.

Barking

Dogs have limited ways of communicating: body language, guttural sounds, howling, whinning and barking. Domestic dogs generally use barking for two specific purposes: one is to rally the troops, and the other is to ward off intruders. Some lone, fearful dogs will call for the troops at the drop of a hat. You can liken them to the behaviour of a lone soldier on point duty that hears the enemy approaching. He feels threatened, he's alone and he's seen a battalion approaching. You can imagine his fear. He needs reinforcements and will do everything to get them there quickly.

Dogs are no different. The more fear they experience, the more they will bark. These dogs are known as nuisance barkers. To address the barking problems, wait for your dog to bark. You must catch it in the act in order for it to comprehend why it is getting corrected. Growling the correction word ('Bah'), simultaneously clap your hands. If your dog persists, use either a water squirter your Bark Busters™ training pillow (available from your nearest Bark Busters™ office, with a lesson), which acts as a focus breaker. Drop it near the dog, growling the correction word as you do. In time the correction word will be all you will need if your dog goes back to its bad habit of barking.

There are, of course, times when you will want your dog to bark, such as when people are entering the property or there is impending danger.

Chewing

Chewing, to a puppy, is like a baby sucking – it is quite normal puppy behaviour. You can rest assured that puppies will do a certain amount of chewing between puppyhood and the end of adolescence. Giving your puppy something to chew on such as a meaty bone or a rubber teething ring can offset a lot of destructive chewing. These items have much the same effect as a dummy for a baby.

Lifting your precious items up out of your puppy's reach can also reduce the amount of damage a puppy can do while in its chewing stage.

Dogs that dominate the household

If you are not a consistent owner in regard to the training and disciplining of your dog, it could be led to believe that it is the pack leader rather than you.

I have met many such dogs that 'rule the roost' because instinct has told them the pack needs a leader and their owner does not appear to be displaying the qualities it takes to be that leader.

Inconsistency confuses a dog. If its behaviour is tolerated one day and not the next this can create an impression that the pack leader is losing touch. In the wild, an ageing pack leader would show signs of inconsistency when the rigours of controlling a pack became too difficult. The warning bells would be heard in the ranks – it's time to challenge for leadership.

Summary:

- Chewing is natural puppy behaviour.
- Provide bones or teething rings for your puppy to chew on.
- Practise good puppy management by protecting your precious items.

Digging

There are several reasons why dogs dig. They can be searching for nutrients, digging to keep warm or cool, or digging because of stress. A pregnant mother dog will dig to make a nest for her brood, frightened dogs will attempt to dig out, or sounds under the ground may entice a dog to dig.

First identify the reason why your dog is digging. If your dog is digging because of a lack of nutrients, you will notice that the digging is close to vegetation. The roots of plants will be exposed and partly eaten.

If your dog is digging for the cool or warmth that the soil provides, the digging will be either near the fence, under the house or under a bush or tree.

If your dog is digging to escape, the digging will be near a fence or a gate and part of the earth under the gate or fence will have been dug out.

When an otherwise well-behaved dog suddenly starts digging, it is due to stress. This will generally occur when you are away from the house.

To establish that a dog is digging because of noises nearby you will need some investigation. Check for anything unusual that might have occurred about the time that your dog began digging. It might be someone using a welder, a builder nearby using a nail gun, a new dog in the neighbourhood, the arrival of a new baby or simply because you have moved to a new home.

The cure for digging is as varied as the causes of the problem. Dogs that are digging for nutrients might require a diet change or could need a mineral supplement added to their diet as well as some raw grated root vegetables. Consult your vet for advice about a mineral supplement.

Dogs that are digging to find warmth and or to get cool should be provided with a sandpit. Place the sandpit near the area where your dog is currently digging. Once your dog accepts it, you will be able to move the sandpit anywhere you like.

If your dog is digging to escape, it's telling you it's not happy with the situation it presently resides in because it needs leadership and you are not providing it. So rethink your training regime. You might need expert advice and assistance. Block off the areas that your dog has already dug by positioning a board that is held in place by driving steel or wooden stakes into the ground. Be prepared for your dog to begin to dig elsewhere. In the meantime, this patch-up job will give you the time needed to commence your dog's training program.

Summary:

- Identify the cause of your dog's digging.
- Provide supplements for any dietary deficiencies.
- Provide a sandpit for the dog that is looking for a warm or cool place.
- Block off all areas where a potential escapist is digging.
- When the reason for digging is stress-related, investigate the cause of the stress.

10

Dealing with fears and phobias

Phobias are triggered by something to which the dog overreacts, such as a storm, traffic, fireworks, other dogs, children or strangers. From that point on, every time the circumstances are the same, the dog will relive the fearful experience.

When it comes to dealing with fears and phobias, you must be firm with your dog. It is tough love, but dogs need to know they have a strong leader. A lack of leadership from their owner only serves to make them more fearful. A dog will begin to feel insecure if it senses that its owner is not a good leader. When it senses this, it feels unprotected, and then its fear turns to panic.

When it comes to dealing with fears and phobias, it is best, where possible, to have your dog on lead, and walk with it near the source of its fear. Give your dog encouragement when it progresses without

hesitation and growl when it reacts in a fearful way. You cannot expect a subordinate dog to cope with a frightening situation if the pack leader won't venture out with it.

Phobia-prone dogs are generally afraid of the unknown. Things that they cannot understand or have never seen before can trigger an overreaction and then their fear escalates to the point where they need to escape. When fear is present, adrenaline enters the bloodstream, preparing the body for fight or flight. The adrenaline dramatically impairs the dog's ability to learn or focus. This phenonomem accounts for the many reports from desperate owners of phobia-prone dogs, where the dogs appeared to be in some sort of trance and were totally unresponsive to their commands.

Fear of storms

The extent of the fear or phobia reaction to storms largely depends on the dog's temperament type. Fearful dogs need strong leadership from their owners to help them cope with their fears.

The dog's fear of discipline is generally overwhelmed by their phobia. A fear of storms is hard to fathom, as we don't expect dogs to fear natural phenomena. However, the instances of 'storm fear' have risen markedly since the 1980s. One theory we have developed to explain this phenomenon at Bark Busters™ is that the phobia could be triggered by a lack of nutrients in the dog's diet. A nutrient deficiency can result in serotonin depletion in the dog's brain, making it overly sensitive to loud noises.

We have achieved some dramatic results by treating dogs traumatised by storms with serotonin. Discuss this treatment option for your dog with your vet.

The best interim treatment we have found is to provide a safe haven for the traumatised dog. A portable den is the best solution. Supplying a kennel with carpet nailed to the walls to reduce the noise level can provide the dog with much-needed security.

The den must be dark, warm and as close to the house as possible. It must be strong and secure and have an equally strong door fitted that can be securely locked at night. The addition of piped music in the den is sometimes helpful. Your dog must be trained to sleep in the den at all other times. The best way to introduce your puppy or dog to its den is to lock it in at night. It must feel safe and secure in its den, a sense which can only be established over time.

Summary:

- Check with your vet for the possibility that your dog is suffering from serotonin depletion.
- Create a haven by introducing a portable den.
- Lock your puppy in its den at night.

Fear of fireworks

The fear of fireworks is another phobia that appears to have surfaced in the last twenty years, reaching epidemic proportions in the last five years. Firework phobia is best treated in the same way as the fear of storms – by supplying a portable den that is dark and warm and near the house.

Speak to your vet about the possibility that your dog is suffering serotonin depletion.

A cap gun can be used to desensitise your puppy to the sound of fireworks. Place your puppy on lead and walk with it around the yard while you fire the cap gun. Correct any silly behaviour, with a 'Bah' and clap, or water squirter. Continue for a couple of weeks or until your puppy pays no attention to the cap gun sounds.

The next step is to place your dog on lead, and begin by accustoming it to noises. Start by clanging something metallic as you walk, gradually building up to where you have an assitant firing a muffled cap gun, and eventually walking your dog while you fire the cap gun this must be carried out very carefully and ceased immediately if your dog shows signs of extreme overreaction. If your dog proves too difficult to handle, contact your nearest Bark Busters representative. Continue this for several minutes until your dog ceases to react to the cap gun or looks for the cheese each time the gun goes off.

Summary:
- Check with your vet for the possibility of serotonin depletion.
- Use a cap gun to desensitise your dog to fireworks.
- Provide a portable den.
- Fire the cap gun while you feed it cheese, until your dog stops reacting to the sound.

Fear of strangers

Some dogs have unrealistic fears of people who are not members of their immediate family. There are several reasons for this phobia. The fear may stem from the fact that the dog wasn't correctly socialised while a puppy, or it may be caused by an inherently undesirable temperament. Some dogs have suffered at the hands of a stranger at some time in the past. The following case history explains how dogs can develop a phobia of strangers.

Case history

The story of Bonaparte, a border collie puppy, demonstrates how human behaviour can mar the normal development of a dog, psychologically affecting it for ever. Jenny had always wanted a border collie and had spent many hours researching the breed and finding the right breeder. She was sure she had covered all the bases to ensure that her puppy grew up without behaviour problems. Bonaparte was a well-bred, lovable, well-adjusted puppy.

Everything went well until the day her husband's friend David came to visit. David did not like dogs as he had been bitten by one when he was a child and had never forgotten the incident.

The instant he saw Bonaparte, he was frozen to the spot. Bonaparte, on seeing David, ran to greet him. Remembering his past experience, David panicked, punching the pup as he approached. Bonapartre squealed in pain, running under the lounge and refusing to come out.

It took Jenny and her husband several hours before they were able to coax him out from under the lounge. They called Bark Busters™ to assist them with the problem. We arrived to find what appeared to be a very frightened dog that wouldn't allow any stranger anywhere near him. His teeth were bared, and he was snarling and barking at us.

Jenny's reaction had been that of a mother to an upset child. She was trying to console Bonaparte by saying, 'It's okay'. We explained that although David had been in the wrong, his actions had also been instinctive and the whole thing was an unfortunate incident. We further explained that it would serve no worthwhile purpose to pander to Bonaparte if we wanted his behaviour to improve.

Jenny immediately began to resist us, saying that she felt sorry for him – it was hurting her to see her beloved puppy so obviously unhappy. We agreed that it was not an ideal situation but if she wanted to change things, then she had to change her reaction to her puppy's behaviour. By consoling him she was actually telling him it was okay to be aggressive to strangers.

We explained that she had to put the reasons for Bonaparte's fear out of her mind and start looking at the problem.

We suggested that Jenny place her puppy on lead each time a visitor arrived and give her a treat , a piece of cheese or dried liver. This way the visitors would represent something pleasant, rather than something to fear.

Bonaparte has moved on and now doesn't dart under the lounge when visitors show up. He might never forget his past bad experience, but his faith in people is slowly being restored.

Summary:
- Any aggression towards strangers must be corrected.
- Do not console any dog or puppy that is displaying aggression, regardless of the cause of the problem.
- A puppy must be correctly socialised.

Fear of children

The fear of children almost always stems from a dog suffering trauma at the hands of a child. The dog will then snap at any child that approaches it in an effort to stop the child's advances.

The difference between the way humans and dogs behave in these instances is people hit with their hands while dogs hit with their teeth. Dogs will snap or bite to ward off a child that has previously hurt them. They can then interpret this to mean that all children pose a threat.

Humans nearly always blame the dog for any aggressive reaction, mainly because the child's behaviour is subtle. Puppies and dogs must be disciplined for any display of aggression, but parents must also take some responsibility in educating children how to behave around dogs.

The following case history highlights how problems between dogs and children can occur.

Case history

Clancy, an eight-week-old rottweiler, was a most adorable, gentle creature when Margaret and Jim bought him as a companion for their three-year-old son Joshua, who was their only child.

Clancy was very patient with Joshua at first, allowing him to carry Clancy everywhere, but as Joshua grew, the pain of being picked up and sometimes dropped became unbearable. He began to hide when Joshua approached, but Joshua was small enough to get into any place where Clancy could hide.

Margaret and Jim could see no wrong in Joshua's actions. They enjoyed seeing the interactions of child and puppy, totally unaware that a big problem was brewing.

Clancy then tried snapping at Joshua as he approached, which did nothing to deter Joshua. He wanted to carry his playmate at any cost. Margaret and Jim became very alarmed at this behaviour from Clancy and rang his breeder. The breeder was at a loss to explain the pup's anti-social behaviour as none of her other puppies had displayed any aggression in the past.

Margaret and Jim were beginning to contemplate sending Clancy back to the breeder when one day, out of the blue, he bit Joshua right on the cheek just below his eye. This was the final straw. Joshua was rushed to hospital and Clancy was taken to the vet to be put to sleep that day.

It was obvious that Clancy had had enough of Joshua's behaviour. He had tried avoidance tactics, he had tried a warning – the snap – used by dogs to warn their adversaries that a bite is on the way if they persist. None of these tactics worked. Clancy had only one more option left to him, and so he took it. The only problem was this natural, instinctive action cost him his life.

Clancy's breeders relayed this story to Bark Busters™. It highlights the reasons dogs may learn to dislike children. The onus of good puppy and child management rests with the dog owner and the child's parents to ensure that no child gets hurt by a dog and no puppy or dog receives drastic punishment.

Summary:

- Dogs hit with their teeth, while humans hit with their hands.
- A puppy that snaps at a child is generally showing signs of fearing the child's advances.
- Children must be educated about how to behave around puppies and dogs.

Fear of other dogs

This problem will occur in puppyhood generally because of incorrect socialisation. Puppies are very impressionable creatures. A dog or puppy from outside the pack should never be allowed to dominate another puppy.

When dogs or puppies are permitted to dominate your puppy you create a situation where your puppy feels it has to either dominate another or be dominated. This feeling creates anxiety in the puppy, which can manifest itself in aggression. The correct grounding for your puppy is important if you wish to prevent aggression from occurring.

Puppies that have already developed this problem will need their owners to assert dominance to stop the behaviour.

Do not wait for the aggression to build, but act the instant your puppy is showing signs of aggression, such as placing its ears forward, tail up, or standing erectly. Correct this aggression by using the 'Bah' and clap technique. Some very determined puppies might need a water squirter or a Bark Busters™ training pillow.

Summary:

- Do not allow your puppy to be dominated by other dogs or puppies outside of its pack.
- Correct any aggressive behaviour while your puppy is still contemplating it.
- Use a water squirter or Bark Busters™ training pillow with a more advanced case of puppy aggression.

Fear of traffic

Puppies should be exposed to traffic from an early age to ensure that fear and phobias do not occur. Traffic can be very frightening for an uninitiated puppy as the sound and movement of the traffic is perceived to be something that is alive. The puppy's fear of something it has never experienced before will grow, adrenaline will enter its bloodstream, and it will feel the urge to run.

Any introduction to traffic should be carried out on lead. Take your puppy to a busy spot near the road, but not too near the kerb, find a spot to sit and spend some time just watching the traffic. Your puppy will need at least several half-hour sessions of just sitting and watching the traffic to assure it that the traffic will do it no harm at this distance.

Any frantic behaviour must be corrected. Do not pity your puppy because you will never solve the problem if you do. Your puppy needs to know that you do not approve of any frantic or undesirable behaviour to demonstrate that it has a strong leader.

Summary:

- It is always best to expose puppies to traffic from an early age.
- Always fit a lead when introducing your puppy to traffic.
- Conduct several half-hour sessions near traffic to accustom your puppy to the traffic.
- Correct any frantic or undesirable behaviour.

11

Dealing with aggression and biting

Instinct and aggression

Contrary to popular belief, most dogs would prefer not to bite humans or attack each other. Given this natural reluctance to bite, why are more and more dogs displaying acts of aggression towards people and other dogs? Daily we hear of new cases of people being maimed or killed by dogs.

A man in Perth, Australia, was charged with murder when his rottweilers killed an elderly woman. In the United States a woman was charged with murder and later had this charge altered to manslaughter when her dogs attacked and killed a young woman.

The reasons for the increase in these types of attacks are numerous. Firstly there are more dogs in our society than ever before. By law we have to keep them isolated, and local councils are constantly introducing tougher legislation to ensure that owners confine their dogs.

In my opinion, such restrictions are largely responsible for the increase in attacks by dogs. In the past, dogs were free to roam and socialise with people and other dogs. Socialised dogs are normally friendly dogs, but isolated dogs can become fearful, which may lead to aggressive behaviour.

Another reason for dog aggression is that the average person does not understand what motivates a dog to attack. They are unaware that their actions might incite canine aggression.

Dogs are unable to think or reason in the same way that humans do – they do not possess human logic. Instead, memory and instinct mostly guide their behaviour.

Often when a dog bites it is reacting from instinct.

Dogs that bite

Most cases of canine aggression are caused by fear. Very few confident dogs will bite. A dog's fear may manifest from a lack of proper socialisation. Dogs that are bred away from suburbia in an environment where strangers or other dogs are rarely seen may become fearful when they meet strangers or other dogs for the first time – it's the fear of the unknown.

Fear is a powerful survival instinct. If something scares a dog, it will do one of two things: run away or stay and fight. This is known as the 'fight or flight' response, which is common to all mammals, including humans.

A dog that has had no contact with strangers or other dogs or one that has experienced a trauma at the hands of a human being or a strange dog is much more likely to attack than a dog that has enjoyed only good experiences.

Some dogs are simply born fearful. This is due to indiscriminate breeding, breeding without much forethought or dogs randomly selecting a partner, resulting in an undesirable temperament being passed down the generations.

Some otherwise well-bred dogs might develop fear due to their environment being void of any social experiences. They live in virtual isolation and so cannot cope when confronted with things outside of their understanding. Others will develop fear because they have no leader, they instinctively know they are not the leader types, and therefore feelings of vulnerability begin to manifest when their owners fail to display leadership qualities. They take matters into their own hands and act to protect themselves.

Case history

We were visiting an animal shelter in Colorado called the Max Fund. There was a dog that had been there three years that was very aggressive and none of the shelter staff could get near the dog other than the ladies who brought its meals. Tucker had remained at the shelter from the time it was a young puppy and had become institutionalised. It was a sad sight to behold and I felt very sorry for the dog. I asked the staff if they would allow us to help the dog and permit me to do some work with him. They agreed and we returned a week later. I sought out a lady who was one of the few people he would trust. I then instructed the lady to enter the cage and I would guide her as to how to solve the dog's aggression problems. I told her that the dog needed to be shown that he did not need to fear people. I asked her to growl 'Bah' and drop a training pillow onto the ground to alter the dog's focus every time he became aggressive to anyone passing his cage.

The transformation was almost immediate, he started to look to the lady for direction each time someone passed his cage, rather than leaping up and down, frothing at the mouth and barking ferociously. Within minutes he was ignoring passersby and instead looking at the lady for guidance. The shelter staff were amazed. They couldn't believe it was the same dog. I then decided it was time I went into the cage, so I threw some liver treats to the back of the cage and as he went to get them, I entered the cage. He appeared quite surprised and I stood perfectly still while he sniffed and assessed me. I continued to feed him by dropping liver treats onto the ground and he stayed near me, forgetting his fear of strangers. It was an exhilarating moment and everyone witnessing the event could not help but be moved. The dog is now going to a new home and Bark Busters™ USA will continue his training.

Territoriality

Territoriality is defined in the *Macquarie Dictionary* as 'the behaviour of an animal in claiming and defending its territory'. A dog's territory is the area that it claims as its own and will defend against intruders.

The ancestors of the modern-day dog had to defend the areas in which they lived and hunted. The territory they chose largely would have depended on its resources. They would have needed shelter from the sun and rain, as well as easy access to a watering hole or spring. Caves or rocks, under which they could dig dens, would probably have been an important factor, providing the female of the species with a suitable place for whelping. This instinct to protect their territory was essential to their survival.

This same instinct to protect territory is still very strong in domestic dogs, even though we provide for most of their needs. If a dog considers an area to be its territory and a strange human being or dog trespasses onto that territory, then they could be in trouble if they don't know the rules.

The size of an area a dog will defend depends on the size of the area the dog has to roam, whether it has free range or is confined to a backyard. The following case history shows how people may be attacked when venturing into a dog's territory and reacting in the wrong way.

Case history

As part of his job, David visited other people's homes on a regular basis. The one thing he disliked intensely about his door-to-door work was dogs. Even though he had two of his own, David was afraid of dogs. He'd had more than one close shave when confronted by them.

David had recently had an operation on his knee and was walking with the aid of a walking stick. On this particular day he was also carrying a large bag. He came to a house that was fully enclosed by a fence, with a large double gate at the entrance. Without any hesitation he went through the gate, closing it behind him. He froze momentarily when he heard a dog bark, but continued down the path, thinking the dog was locked inside. At that moment, a bull terrier emerged from under the house. David stopped in his tracks; the hairs stood up on the back of his neck and he broke into a cold sweat.

He wanted to run, but the gate was closed and too far away, he knew he would never make it. The dog trotted up to him, barking.

Fearing an attack, David thrust his bag straight into the unsuspecting dog's face. The dog grabbed it in his jaws and the two were locked in a tussle.

David tried unsuccessfully to get his bag back. Although his instinct was to get out of there, he was not leaving without his bag. No matter how hard he pulled, the dog would not let go.

Up until this point David had not received any injuries, other than to his pride. He looked around but there was no one in sight, no one to help him out of the predicament he was in. Mustering his courage, David decided to take action.

Lifting his walking stick above his head, he brought it down forcefully on the bull terrier's head. The dog let go of the bag and attacked him with all the force and frenzy it could muster. His worst nightmares had come true – he was under attack. The dog went berserk, attacking David with such force that he was knocked to the ground. The dog was now on top of him. David attempted to cover his face, but the dog was biting every limb. David was fighting for his life.

Suddenly the dog's owner appeared from inside the house, and grabbing the dog's collar, pulled the dog off David, and then rang an ambulance.

David was taken to hospital suffering from shock and 47 puncture wounds to his arms, legs and torso.

The dog's owner was also in shock and at a loss to explain the attack as his dog had never bitten anyone before.

You might think that this was a particularly aggressive, unprovoked attack, and that the dog should have been declared dangerous and put to sleep. The attack was certainly vicious, but let's take a moment to consider the situation from the dog's point of view.

Here was a normal, friendly dog that always barked as a stranger entered his yard. A dog's bark is used to call the pack or ward the intruder off, so is not an absolute prelude to an attack. The dog had trotted up to David barking, then a bag was thrust in its face, and the dog had grabbed the bag, no doubt to ensure that the bag was not thrust into its face again. David then attacked the dog with a walking stick in its own yard.

How would you feel if someone entered your home and when you called out 'Who's there?' a stranger approached and thrust a bag into your face, which you grabbed hold of to ensure that they didn't do that again? Then, without warning, if the stranger hit you over the head with a walking stick, how would you react?

Unfortunately a dog cannot stop to ask questions, it can only draw on its instinct. Instinct tells the dog that when in danger it has only two options, either to run away or fight. A dog in defence of its own territory, when threatened, is more likely to fight. To run would be surrendering the territory to someone else.

Food aggression

In the wild, a dog's survival largely depended on its food supply. The dog's ability to protect its food was literally the difference between life and death. Puppies that did not push and shove to get the best morsels or defend their meal usually perished. Domestic dogs learn as puppies that they need to push and fight to get the lion's share of the food, especially if in a large litter of puppies. In situations where puppies of a large litter are forced to eat from the one bowl, they are encouraged to growl and be aggressive over their food. This pushing and shoving creates panic and stress in the puppies, leading them to believe that if they don't protect their food they will go hungry.

Because dogs are creatures of habit this pushing and growling can very well continue when they go to a new home. Their need to protect their food continues, so if the owner gets in their way, they could very well be bitten.

The best way to deal with a puppy or dog that is protective of its food bowl is to dispense with the bowl altogether. This usually solves the problem very quickly. Other techniques can be to either scatter the food, making it harder for the dog to protect its meal, which diffuses the situation.

By hand-feeding your dog or puppy you can also diffuse its need to protect its food. Hand-feeding means offering a bone or morsel of food, and then allowing the dog to finish eating before you offer the next piece, and so on until the meal is finished. This allows you to monitor the process. You can assess if any bones are left lying around that the dog might want to protect. The feeding of soft, easily managed bones, which can be consumed quickly, is the safest way to ensure no bones are left lying around.

Case history

Many years ago while I was managing an RSPCA shelter, a woman brought in an aged German shepherd named Sasha. The lady was distraught and asked me if I would euthanise her dog immediately. The dog appeared to be very healthy, showing no obvious signs of why such drastic action would be necessary.

I asked her why she wanted to have the dog put down. She explained that she loved Sasha very much and that the dog had once saved her life when she almost drowned in the surf. However, the previous day, her 14-year-old son had entered their backyard and attempted to lean his bike against a tree, something he did on a regular basis, but this time Sasha had attacked him, inflicting severe wounds to his face. The whole family was in shock. None of them felt they could trust Sasha ever again.

My inquiring, investigative mind would not let the matter rest, so I prodded the woman for more information.

Had Sasha ever bitten anyone before? No.

Could she think of any reason for the attack? No.

Had Sasha known it was her son that was entering the property? This time the answer was 'yes'. The woman's son had told her that Sasha had greeted him in her usual way, happy and with tail wagging. She only became aggressive when he approached the tree.

This information prompted my next question: was Sasha protective of her food? The woman looked puzzled. Was she aggressive if anyone went near her food?

The woman appeared not to understand what I was getting at, though she nodded. 'Yes, she would snarl at you if you went near her food or if she had a bone, and we all knew that, so we stayed well away when she was eating. But this had nothing to do with food as she was not eating at the time.'

At this point I took hold of Sasha's lead and said to the woman, 'I want you to go home and dig around that tree, because I think you will unearth the reason your son was attacked. I won't do anything with Sasha until you get back to me with your findings.

The woman returned an hour later and as she began to speak tears filled her eyes. 'You were right,' she said. 'I found a bone I had given her the other day, buried right where my son's bike was standing. What should I do? My husband and family are adamant that they do not want to take any more chances with Sasha. My son has 15 stitches in his face and he is scarred for life.'

'The choice has to be yours. I can only tell you why it happened and give you advice on how to prevent it from happening again.'

Sasha didn't go home that day because her owner was unable to find the strength to trust her again, so she was put to sleep.

The RSPCA could not pass on a dog of Sasha's age or reputation as other people could have been at risk. She needed specialist training and this was better carried out by those she had loved and trusted for so long.

Self-preservation

Self-preservation simply means looking after yourself and protecting yourself from harm. When it comes to the animal kingdom, the instinct for self-preservation is very powerful.

An animal will protect itself tenaciously when it feels threatened. The only time it will ignore its own well-being is when protecting its offspring. In this case, animals have been known to try to draw predators away from their offspring using themselves as bait or they will attack viciously, risking injury.

When citing self-preservation as a reason for domestic dog attacks, we have to keep in mind that we are dealing with a simple thinking creature that has no understanding of the ways of the human world even while living closely with humans.

I am almost certain that if Sasha had known that by attacking her mistress's son she was signing her own death warrant, she would not have done it. She was merely acting instinctively to preserve her life, not destroy it. Obviously she had no idea where her actions that day would lead.

With that in mind, the following case history tells the story of a dog that attacked because it felt its life was in danger.

Case history

A labrador called Chester, who spent a great deal of his life tied to a kennel, was the perpetrator of an horrendous attack upon his owner's next-door neighbour. The neighbour had hit Chester with a stick on many occasions, thrown rocks at him and hosed him over the fence when Chester's owners were out, all in an attempt to quell Chester's frantic barking. Chester had come to fear the man, but had no way of avoiding the constant onslaught.

All efforts by the neighbour to quell his barking only made him bark more frantically out of fear for his life.

The tables were turned dramatically one Christmas Eve when the neighbour was a guest at Chester's owner's house. Having had one two many, he staggered into the yard to relieve himself, forgetting all about Chester.

Lying inside his kennel, hidden by the darkness, Chester must have recognised the man's footsteps and voice as he mumbled something to himself while he fumbled with his clothing. Chester tensed himself, no doubt fearing another beating.

Waiting until the man was within reach of his chain, Chester pounced, grabbing the man on the buttocks. The man lurched forward in pain, freeing himself from the dog's jaws, but Chester then sunk his teeth into the man's calf muscle, and this time he was not letting go. The man fell to the ground screaming. Suddenly the light went on in the garden, and Chester's owner appeared on the scene.

It took the owner and two other guests to finally prise the man's leg from the dog's jaws. The man refused all requests to take him to the hospital and he would not hear of Chester being punished for the attack. He said it was his fault and a few days later even confessed to Chester's owner how he had been treating the dog.

Sadly, a week later, Chester was put to sleep by his owner, who felt he was too dangerous and unpredictable. Even in light of what he had been told, no amount of pleading by the neighbour could convince Chester's owner to give him a stay of execution.

Protection of mate, offspring or owner

Many dog attacks occur because people or other dogs either come too close to whatever the dog is protecting or inadvertently threaten one of the things the dog holds dear. In the wild, a dog relies heavily on the pack for its survival. The pack provides food, companionship, social structure and security. It is therefore in the dog's own interest to protect pack members. Because a dog looks upon its owner as part of the pack, it can become protective of them and other members of the family if it believes they are being threatened.

Most mothers, whether human or animal, have a natural inclination to protect their offspring. This instinct is nature's way of protecting that particular species. I remember many years ago trying to lead my German shepherd Monty down the garden to see his puppies and the reluctance he displayed as we approached the kennel where my female Sheba was nursing Monty's offspring. No one was more surprised than I was that day when she flew out of the kennel and attacked him. He knew instinctively that he would not be welcome. Sheba was very happy for me, the pack leader, to visit her puppies, but for Monty it was out of bounds. The dog's world can appear to be cruel and uncaring, but Sheba was simply protecting her puppies because she knew instinctively that some male dogs kill male puppies at birth.

Medical reasons for aggressive behaviour

In much the same way that someone's personality can change because of certain medications or medical problems, so too can a dog's.

Some medications can alter the chemistry of the brain, making the dog behave in a different way. At Bark Busters™ we have seen dogs that have been on medication, which, when discontinued, causes the dog to suffer withdrawal symptoms. Although I'm not a vet, I have spent a lifetime observing dogs' behaviour. To me the signs of medication withdrawal in these dogs were self-evident, because previously well-behaved animals suddenly became unpredictable, even attacking their owners.

Distemper can lead to dramatic personality changes because the disease attacks the brain and can cause the afflicted dog to hallucinate. Dogs can also become aggressive due to hormonal changes in the body, such as when a bitch is in season. Brain tumours and rabies (not found in Australia) can similarly affect a dog's personality.

Any personality change should be regarded as an indication that something is not quite right with the dog. Dogs don't have moods like humans, so if something happens out of the ordinary, as described in the following case history, consult a vet.

Case history

I was asked to assess the behaviour of a springer spaniel called Bouncer when his owner, Teresa, was becoming very concerned about his recent unpredictable temperament.

Teresa explained that Bouncer would be sleeping one minute then would jump up and bite one of the family when they walked past his bed, then go back to sleep as if nothing had happened.

There were other unexplained behaviours such as barking at an empty space in the house and growling at lounge cushions. Teresa said that Bouncer seemed like a completely different dog to the one she had always known.

Teresa couldn't think of anything that could have caused the problem. There were times when Bouncer appeared to be his normal healthy self, then something would snap in his brain and the weird behaviour would begin.

I listened carefully to Teresa's description of the things Bouncer had been doing, then we went out into the yard to see him. He came up wagging his tail, his tongue lolling in his mouth. He appeared to be a very friendly, pleasant and agreeable dog.

I decided to put him on lead to take him through some basic exercises to assess his reactions. He became very excited when I produced the lead. I had planned to walk him around the garden first to see just how he would respond to me. He was very affectionate; I began to see what Teresa was talking about. Here was a loving dog that was not not normally aggressive, so there had to be an explanation for his peculiar behaviour.

Suddenly Bouncer did something very unusual – he hooked both of his front paws around my legs as if to stop me from moving forward. I had seen other dogs do this before but they were usually not lead trained, so this was something different.

He seemed to be trying to tell me something. I crouched down and patted his head, fondling his soft ears. He snuggled into me, I looked into his eyes, and what I saw there told me that there was something seriously wrong with this dog. It is difficult to describe; the dog's eyes appeared glazed and staring as if in a trance. His coordination was also not that of a normal dog.

I turned to Teresa and told her she should take Bouncer to a vet as soon as possible. I thought that he either had a minor dose of distemper, which had left him brain damaged or a brain tumour. I'm not a vet, and my opinion was based on intuition more than anything else.

Bouncer never displayed any aggression to me, but I knew that things with him were not quite right.

Teresa rang a few days later to tell me that Bouncer had been diagnosed with an inoperable brain tumour. She told me his condition had worsened, to such a degree that no one was game to venture into the yard, so Teresa had made a tough decision and had him put to sleep.

I shed a silent tear when I remembered the way Bouncer seemed to be trying to tell me that he was suffering; I will never forget the look in that dog's eyes.

Although cases such as this one are rare, they do occur. I have heard of at least five cases in the last year, all of which resulted in the dog being put to sleep.

Hormonal reasons for aggression

Dogs can become more aggressive during puberty when their body starts to produce the sex hormones. The desexing of a male dog can assist with this type of aggression but only in the male of the species. Females when desexed can become more aggressive.

It's the male hormone testosterone that is responsible for the onset of adolescent aggression. This is usually directed at other male dogs, but has been known to be directed at males in the family, especially the young adolescent males.

Both male and female dogs, like humans, are made up of both male and female hormones. The males have predominantly high levels of testosterone with a small amount of progesterone; the female, on the other hand, has predominantly progesterone, with a small amount of testosterone.

The reason females can become aggressive when desexed is due to the fact that it mostly removes the female hormones, leaving the male hormones that are responsible for the aggressive tendencies.

Male dogs when desexed have the male hormones largely removed, leaving the female hormones that make the dog more compliant.

Are certain breeds more aggressive?

I am often asked if there are certain breeds that are more aggressive than others or that are more likely to attack. I believe that it's really the deed not the breed that we should be targeting. People need to be better informed about the best way to prevent their dog from becoming aggressive.

Dogs are basically the same. Some breeds were developed to have strong jaws and fearless temperaments, but these traits can be directed towards productive things rather than negative outcomes.

We often hear media reports about attacks by particular breeds that are deemed dangerous, but we never seem to hear about the other dog attacks that make up a larger proportion of these incidents: 'Chihuahua attacks man', 'Poodle maims child'. Such headlines do not make for sensational news.

It is obvious that if a large dog attacks someone then the injuries will be more serious then if a chihuahua attacked them, but I believe that any dog can be provoked to attack, given a particular set of circumstances. Take Sasha and the bull terrier's stories as examples. They were the most adorable dogs and they might have gone through their lives without any problems if the unfortunate events described in their case histories had not occurred.

A survey conducted in South Australia listed the following breeds as those most responsible for attacks on children:

- American pit bull terrier
- English bull terrier
- German shepherd
- Staffordshire bull terrier
- Rottweiler
- Mastiff
- Doberman

As you read this book, you will notice that some of these breeds feature in the stories about aggression. However, I am not convinced that this means they are more dangerous than any other breeds. Indeed, the figures could just reflect the fact that they are amongst the most popular breeds, therefore statistically responsible for a greater proportion of attacks.

It is my belief that aggression in a dog has far less to do with its breed than it has to do with its upbringing, initial training or whether the owner is responsible about dog ownership.

There is also a trend for some people to select these strong, formidable-looking breeds as guard dogs or have them trained to be aggressive. They are also the breeds of dogs portrayed as aggressive in movies. Therefore their image is already tarnished. You would never see a poodle or chihuahua being used as a guard dog, except perhaps in a comedy. Sometimes the law-makers are not in full receipt of the facts when they decide to place bans on certain breeds.

Dogs that show aggression to other dogs

There are several reasons for dogs being aggressive to other dogs. As mentioned, one reason can be the surge of testosterone in the male dog's system, which normally takes effect at approximately six months of age. Where the aggression is definitely identified to be due to the hormonal levels, the aggressive tendencies will normally start to wane in most male dogs at approximately four years of age.

You can liken this occurrence to the way in which young human males are more likely to pick a fight during adolescence, calming down as they mature, and preferring to walk away from a fight.

Desexing will also fix the hormonal aggression, once the hormones have left the body. Hormones can take anywhere up to a couple of months to completely leach out of the body.

Desexing will not fix aggression if the cause of the aggression is not hormonal.

Stopping a dogfight

One of the most common situations in which people get bitten is when attempting to break up a dogfight. A fighting dog has no conscience; it is just as likely to bite you, as it is to bite its opponent. Even usually placid dogs have been known to bite their owners when they attempted to break up a fight.

Trying to break up a fight by physically intervening is highly dangerous and should *never* be attempted.

Some dogs have been destroyed by court order because a member of the public was bitten when trying to intervene in a dogfight. I do not agree with this type of justice. Dogs in a fight cannot be held responsible for their actions; they are acting on adrenaline and instinct.

As a very young child at school, I witnessed a large dog beating up on a small one. My love of dogs made me act to protect the little dog. I ran and scooped up the little dog into my arms, and as I did so, the bigger dog leapt at me in an effort to get at the little dog again. I turned away to protect the dog from attack and was savaged on the arm for my troubles. That was the last time I intervened in that way.

The best method

When you physically intervene in a dog attack, you appear to the dog to also be in the fight, so you only add to the ferocity of the fight when you become involved physically.

The best technique for breaking up a fight is to remain out of the fight, but use a 'focus breaker'. Water has the ability to break a dog's focus when it is in a fight. It generally has to be a large amount of water, such as water from a hose or a bucket of water. Some determined dogs might need a large tarpaulin or blanket thrown over them to make them quit.

Dog-proofing children

It is vital that all parents, teachers and carers know in what situations dogs represent a real danger to the children in their care. The safety of our children must be paramount in our minds. It is our responsibility to teach them simple, easy-to-remember hints on how to act when around dogs.

Many of the techniques that children are encouraged to use nowadays are potentially dangerous. Some safety programs advocate such tips as: ask the owner before you pat a strange dog; make a fist with your fingers and present the back of your clenched fist to the dog; if attacked by a dog, stare into its eyes. The same programs promote getting children to feed and discipline dogs. No child should ever be encouraged to discipline a dog.

I believe that all of these things are more likely to encourage a dog to bite than prevent it from happening. For example, advising a child to ask a dog owner before they pat a strange dog is dangerous on several counts. Not only are many people bitten when trying to pat a dog, but also, as we have seen from the case histories, most dog owners cannot accurately predict what their dogs will do in a particular situation. Children are encouraged to make a fist to present to a dog. Why? Are they saying that the dog is likely to bite the fingers if they are protruding? If that is the case, why encourage children to take such risks? It is better to teach them to never pat strange dogs.

Protecting your children from dog attack

Because of their diminutive height, which makes it easy for dogs to bite them on the face, children are at a much greater risk than adults of serious injury if attacked by a dog.

Children are also more vulnerable, as far as a dog is concerned, because they have no pack status. In the dog's eyes, the child has the same status as a puppy. Dogs think nothing of disciplining a puppy that breaches protocol or steps out of line and would have no qualms about attacking a child who breached protocol.

Children are more impulsive than adults, so they are more likely to cuddle or pat a dog. This not only places children at risk of attack from strange dogs but also from their own dog.

Children must be taught to show respect for dogs. Children and dogs must be monitored at all times to ensure that potential problems are addressed early on.

Children should never discipline a dog

Children under 12 years of age should never be allowed to discipline a dog. As previously mentioned, dogs view children the same way they view puppies. Puppies have no pack status in the dog's eyes. Adult dogs have no reservations about disciplining puppies. Some growl and snap when a puppy jumps on their head or oversteps the mark. A child trying to discipline a dog will more than likely be bitten for their insolence.

Children are at greater risk of attack than puppies because children do not know the 'pack rules'.

Case history

My doberman Kaydee was recently introduced to my friend's puppy, Cobber. On meeting Kaydee, the puppy immediately jumped up at her face. Kaydee jumped up too, snapping at Cobber, who rolled over onto his back, indicating to Kaydee that it was not threatening her hierarchy. It stayed in that position until she had finished, not moving a muscle. She snapped and growled at the pup. Although it squealed in fear, the amazing thing was that she did not touch it at all. Instead she snapped at each side of its head several times. The whole performance was one of 'show'. Kaydee was just dishing out the dog's disciplinary action for juveniles – the puppy was being shown the protocol.

From that day on, whenever Cobber saw Kaydee again, he would lower his head and grovel past, letting her know that she had his respect.

Unfortunately if a dog tried to discipline a child in the same way, the child might be seriously injured. Children, not understanding the dog's law, might panic if a dog attacked the way Kaydee had and would immediately try to get back up or run away. Both actions could be fatal.

Puppies are aware of the protocol. By freezing their actions and lying motionless they avoid injury. If they tried to fight back the attack would continue and they would be seriously injured.

What to do if you are attacked

By watching a dog's reactions to other dogs I have learnt how to avoid being bitten during an attack. By emulating the freezing of movement that dogs do to avoid serious injury, you can defuse an attack by a dog.

If we want to avoid an attack by a dog we need to make sure that our body language sends the right message. Many people believe that you should submit to a dog that might bite by either crouching down to eye level or lying on the ground. However, by submitting in the way a subordinate dog would, you are placing yourself in extreme danger – the dog could easily bite your face and neck.

If the dog knocks you to the ground, then by all means stay down, curl yourself into a ball, and freeze your action, but don't place yourself in such a vulnerable situation if it's unnecessary.

There is also a popular misconception that you should, on meeting a dog, offer it the back of your hand. A dog that has been hit with a hand in the past might think that the approaching hand is going to hit it

and could snap at it. I wish I had dollar for all of those people who have told me that they were bitten when attempting to do this.

The initial introduction to any dog should be carried out on the dog's terms. Rather than offer the dog the back of your hand, keep your hands locked in front of you and close to your body. Allow the dog to sniff and assess you. Dogs prefer to approach you on their terms. Rush the introductory process and you'll soon suffer the consequences.

Stand Right No Bite™

When you stand still freezing the action you are imitating the behaviour of a dog that is neither aggressive nor submissive – it's a passive pose. It is designed to lead the dog to believe that you are neither a pushover nor are you a threat.

This type of body language is the safest way to deal with all types of aggression. I have used this technique on hundreds of aggressive dogs that had previously attacked and bitten other people who had used traditional methods.

I have long believed in this non-aggressive approach to warding off dog attacks. I call this method the Stand Right No Bite™ technique. My husband Danny and I developed it after many years of research and personal experience while working with aggressive dogs.

The basics of the Stand Right No Bite™ technique are as follows:

- Do not pat a strange dog.
- Do not stare at any dog.
- If attacked, stand completely still, and freeze your actions.
- Do not make any threatening or provocative movements.
- If a dog knocks you to the ground, roll into a ball and stay down.

You should never fight back with any dog, especially if attacked by one of the fighting breeds, you have no chance of winning. The dog could inflict fatal injuries.

Understanding the dog's reactions

When you employ the techniques of Stand Right No Bite™ as described above, you will find that there will be several different reactions from the dog, depending on its personality and level of dominance.

Some dogs will rush at you, barking and growling, then will stop short by approximately 400 millimetres. If you attempt to run or move, they will attack. While others will keep coming and will punch you with their nose attempting to elicit a reaction from you, if you react by either kicking out or backing up, they will bite. If you stand totally still, they generally won't attack you.

Others will grab you, but these are generally fear biters that will attack from behind. Often they will grab your leg and hold on. The best way to deal with this is to stand your ground, freeze the action and wait the dog out. If you pull away, the dog will definitely tear flesh.

A dog once grabbed my leg in an attack. It just stood there waiting for me to move, and it was like a Mexican stand-off. I turned my head and growled 'Bah' down at the dog without turning my body. It let go of my leg. I had no marks whatsoever on my leg when the dog released me.

Case history

Todd was reading a meter at a client's house when he was attacked from behind by a bull terrier, which grabbed his leg. Todd later told me that if he hadn't attended a Stand Right No Right™ lecture, his first reaction would have been to jump forward or run, and this, he believed, would have caused him serious injury.

Instead he stood totally still, calling out for the owner to get the dog off him. Neither the dog owner nor Todd could believe that the dog had left no mark on his leg at all.

Those at risk

For 14 years I have conducted extensive research into the causes of dog aggression and dog attacks. My investigations have been carried out overseas as well as in Australia. I have discovered that the people most at risk of dog attack are those who have a fear of dogs. The dogs most likely to bite are those that fear humans. When you get this combination it's a dangerous cocktail for a serious dog attack.

Case history

When I popped into a video shop recently to return some tapes, there was a large female Rottweiler waiting in the doorway for her owner. I was in a hurry and brushed past the dog, not seeing her at first. She jumped up in shock. I faced her as I froze my actions, allowing her to sniff and assess me, after which she appeared to settle. I moved off, keeping my eye on her, knowing that a fearful dog might try to have a sneaky bite as I walked away if I were to inadvertently take my eyes off it.

This could very easily have turned into an attack situation, if I had been the type of person who was fearful of dogs and had reacted adversely – the way my cleaner reacted the day she met my two wonderful dogs. They had approached her the way they approach everyone – they rushed up to her confidently, looking for a pat. She reacted with fear, the same way the rottweiler reacted to me.

She jumped about, raising her hands in the air and moving away each time that they tried to sniff and assess her. The dogs seemed to be thinking,

'Who is this strange creature? Why is it reacting this way?' They were so accustomed to being around dog-lovers that they just didn't know how to deal with this behaviour.

Imagine if my cleaner had met the rottweiler – that could have been a recipe for disaster.

If you have a natural fear of dogs, the best thing to do when approached by a dog is to stand totally still and allow it to sniff you. Be aware that a dog will have to touch you with its nose to do this. Do not move away until the dog has lost interest. Do not show fear by backing away. It is not necessary to pat or try to make friends; just wait for the dog to move off then back away slowly, keeping your eye on the dog without staring.

All dogs must be approached with care. Never assume a dog will not bite. Always wait for it to accept you first, allowing it to sniff you until it loses interest, only then should you move off.

Tips for the elderly

Elderly people are almost as vulnerable to dog attacks as young children. Whenever I hear of a dog attack, it upsets me, but nothing upsets me more than to hear about attacks on the very young or the very old.

If you have an elderly person in the family or if you have a neighbour who feels vulnerable to dog attack, explain to them about how to react if attacked. Run them through the pointers or lend them this book. They must know to stand still if a dog runs at them, and if they are knocked to the ground, they must remain down and roll into a ball until help arrives.

Aggression when the owner is present

When a dog enters a new home, it does not look upon its owner as a different species but another dog. It sees itself as part of the pack whether there is only one owner or a whole family. As time passes, it starts to work out where it fits in the pecking order.

It stands to reason that a potential biter will be far more confident when with its owner than when alone.

My dog Kaydee is a gentle doberman, but even she can become aggressive when circumstances are right, such as the day she stumbled upon me in the bathroom trying on a hat. She did not recognise me and froze on the spot, growling at me. Hearing her growls, my husband came running. Now she was backed up by the pack, Kaydee went into action, rushing at me. I stood still and whispered her name. She stopped and sniffed at me, then wagged her tail.

How the dog's senses affect aggression

In the above story about Kaydee, you might very well wonder why my own dog didn't recognise me. Dogs do not recognise people the way we do. If you have ever seen a pack of greyhounds chasing a lure, you will know that the greyhounds cannot see that it is not a real animal, but a mechanical lure. The dogs chase after it with great excitement. If they were to catch up and sniff it, they would immediately realise that it's not real, however they chase after the lure because its movement makes it appear real.

Dogs learn to recognise their owners, people and other dogs through several different processes. One method of recognition is scent. Each individual person or creature has a unique scent, so there are no two creatures that smell the same to the dog.

Dogs also recognise people via the sound of their voices. No two voices sound alike to a dog.

Another way dogs recognise people, especially those they spend a great deal of time with is from the regular habits of that person. They drive the same car, they come out of the same room, they walk a certain way, and they wear particular clothes.

If the owner alters their appearance (even slightly as I did with the hat), approaches from a different route or turns up in a different car, the dog is likely to bark at them until they hear their voice or they approach close enough to scent them.

Dogs' eyesight

The dog has limited vision so they don't see things the way humans do. Dogs are colour blind and possess what's known as binocular vision, which means they can sees things off in the distance better than they can sees things up close.

The reason nature blessed dogs with this type of vision is linked to their survival. During the war the armed forces used people who were colour blind to view aerial maps to assist them in spotting camouflaged enemy vehicles and airfields.

I believe that colour blindness is necessary for dogs because it enables them to hunt small prey and spot moving animals despite their camouflage. Binocular vision makes it easier for the dog to see over great distances, again assisting its hunting ability.

The dog is a sophisticated hunting machine, but its limited vision creates problems when trying to see things up close. Then it relies heavily on its sense of smell. You need to be aware of a dog's limitations when you are dealing with it, because if you mistakenly believe that its eyesight is as good as human eyesight, you may blunder into a situation that could escalate out of control.

The dog's sense of smell

If you compare the dog's sense of smell to that of a human, you could say that the dog's sense of smell is 400 per cent greater than ours. Dogs have 200 million olfactory cells compared to our 5 million. Spread out, our nasal membrane covers the area of a postage stamp, whereas a dog's would cover the size of an A4 sheet of paper. Dogs also have a much larger area in the brain for processing scents that are received and dissolved by their olfactory cells. Dogs also possess what's known as the 'Jacobson's organ', which is positioned behind their front teeth, allowing them to smell and taste chemical scents.

The truth about scent

Scent is given off by all living creatures. Dogs have evolved to locate and identify other dogs, fellow pack members, as well as prey by the use of their scenting powers.

Body scent comprises the individual odours created by dead skin cells; the average sized person sheds two million cells per day.

Body scent is found in two forms: ground and foot scent, which the dog locates when very close to the source; and air scent during breezy or windy conditions, which lifts the scent from the ground and disperses it much like smoke in the wind.

Although it's clear to see that the dog's sense of smell is far superior to that of a human being, there are still misconceptions about the dog's scenting ability. Some people, because of what they have heard about the dog's scense of smell, credit the dog with super powers that it does not possess. They believe that a dog can scent them from across the room or even from down the street, which is definitely not the case.

It is true that dogs have an amazing ability to follow and determine scents way beyond our ability, but they still have their limitations. Dogs cannot scent a human approaching downwind of them; they need to get very close to people in order to identify them. They do not suck in the air and think, 'That's a human being, it's Billy from down the street'. They would only be able to scent Billy if there was a breeze blowing from behind him in their direction, otherwise they would have to approach Billy and sniff him.

To test this theory you can conduct an experiment with your own dog. Leave the room and have someone hold the dog while you change into a long dark coat, putting on a hat and a pair of sunglasses. Now re-enter the room without speaking, stand totally still, and have your assistant release the dog. Wait for your dog's reaction. If your dog comes over to you, watch how close it has to approach to scent you before it realises who you are. Your dog won't recognise you and will need to sniff you to ascertain who you are.

Given these facts about the dog's senses and their limitations, it's surprising that more people don't fall victim to dog attack. I believe it is up to us as human beings to be the responsible ones in the relationship.

Handling dogs safely: a guide for professionals

If handling dogs is part of your job, the likelihood of being bitten is high and the rules are somewhat different from those we have covered so far.

The environment in which you might be dealing with the dog plays a large part in whether or not a dog is likely to attack you. Have you entered the dog's territory?

Are you in an open or confined space?

Are you examining the dog on a table where it is at eye level or on the ground?

To cover these different situations, I have divided this chapter into two sections. Section 1 is for rangers, vets, kennel hands, groomers and the like and section 2 is for those of you in the service industry, meter

rate your dog's behavior at www.barkbusters.com

readers, postal workers and door-to-door representatives, those people whose daily work brings them into contact with dogs but who don't have to handle them.

Guidelines for vets, vet nurses, kennel hands, animal shelter workers and groomers

Approaching a dog correctly

When approaching a strange dog and its owner, it is advisable to allow the dog to assess you first. As you approach, don't stare at the dog or attempt to pat or touch it. Talk to the owner calmly, allowing the dog to sniff you if it wants to. Keep your hands in front of you and held close to your body.

Sometimes it is better to ignore the dog until it shows you that it has accepted you. Dogs need time to sniff and assess you, otherwise they will bite. Most people are bitten because they try to rush the initial meeting process with dogs. If a dog is not going to accept you readily it will usually withdraw or try to hide behind its owner. Pushing a dog too far at this stage by persistently trying to make friends will only add to the dog's fear. If you are talking to the owner in a calm manner, the dog will be more likely to accept you because the owner does.

A dog that accepts you will usually push its head up under your hand for a pat. Do not attempt to pat the dog before it has given you this sign.

Taking a dog from the owner

There are special ways to handle dogs that lessen the risk of attack. I discovered very early on in my career that it is best if the owner hands the dog to me, rather than if I take the dog from the owner. This often makes the difference between whether or not the dog will try to bite me.

An RSPCA worker was very nearly bitten on the face by a little dog in its owner's arms. The only thing that saved her was her glasses. When the dog snapped at her face, it hit her glasses instead. I later took this dog from the owner, but this time I asked her to hand the dog to me, rather than reaching over and taking it from her arms. The dog looked astonished, but it made no attempt to bite me.

The same tactic applies if you are dealing with a dog on lead. I was grabbed on the shoulder by a mastiff one day when I attempted to take its lead from the owner. Fortunately, the dog did not bite me; I stood totally still and waited for the owner to release the dog's grip on me.

When a dog's owner hands you the dog (or lead), the dog feels that its owner approves of what's going on and usually does not resist, thereby greatly reducing the risk of attack.

Case history

Neil had been working in a grooming parlour for many years, and was puzzled as to why dogs sometimes bit him. I asked him to tell me how he acts when a dog is brought into the salon so I could ascertain exactly what he is doing wrong.

Neil said he always approaches a dog from the front, and pats it or takes its lead from the owner and tries to lead it away. Mostly this works, but some dogs aren't comfortable with this approach and will snap at or bite him.

I explained to Neil that he needs to give the dog time to accept him and that he should ask the owner to pass the lead to him rather than taking the lead from the owner, which may make the dog think that he is being taken away against the owner's will.

I also pointed out that he might be behaving too provocatively by staring at the dog as he approaches. This places a dog under pressure and could encourage it to attack to protect itself.

Examining dogs

Again, it is important to give the dog time to accept you by talking to the owner first and allowing the dog to sniff you. Also bear in mind that the dog might have had an unpleasant experience during a similar examination in the past.

I believe most veterinary examination tables are too high, giving the patient a height advantage over the examiner and thereby increasing the risk of an attack. Wherever possible, try to conduct the examination with the dog standing on the ground. This will give you a definite height advantage.

It is advisable to muzzle the dog if examining its eyes, because dogs feel very threatened when you stare into their eyes.

Always keep your eye on the dog – its body language will reveal what it is thinking. A dog that is likely to bite in this situation will be focused on you, tight-lipped with a very tense body and looking for a way out. A dog that is relaxed and unconcerned about you will have a relaxed posture and might be panting.

Dealing with a dog that feels cornered

If a dog is cornered, it will feel threatened, and because most veterinary examination rooms are quite small, the risk of a dog feeling trapped in these circumstances is high. Try to involve the owner as much as possible by getting them to hold their dog for you. Try to assess if they are confident and capable of holding the dog firmly. A frightened owner is more likely to cause an attack as the dog will feed off their fear and may bite you.

Handling dogs in cages

A frightened dog shut in a small cage will usually feel threatened. If you need to administer treatment to the dog or remove it from the cage and the cage is at face height, the dog will have the height advantage and therefore the upper hand. When dealing with dogs in this situation, stand on a chair or stepladder to give yourself the advantage.

Removing a dog from a car

When transporting a dog, it is imperative to secure the dog in the back of the car with a harness or a dog safety belt. If neither of these is available, it is possible to use two leads attached to the dog's collar, which can be tied to the seat belt anchors or handles above the window on either side of the car. This prevents the dog from becoming tangled in the lead as well as making it easier to control. When you remove the dog from the car, you are able to take hold of one lead while the other secures the dog. If a dog should jump at you, hold the lead at arm's length – this will protect you from any snapping teeth. Whenever possible, it's better for the owner to tie the dog in the car.

Make sure you have a doggy treat with you when collecting and dropping off dogs. Simply throw the food at a dog's feet if it becomes aggressive and wait for its mood to change.

When removing a dog from the back of a van, remember the importance of height advantage. You might be better off climbing into the van and asserting this advantage than staying outside and trying to remove the dog that way.

Finally, bear in mind that the dog you are dealing with might feel frightened or trapped. It may even be car-protective, as illustrated in the following case history.

Case history

When I was working for the RSPCA, the police contacted me asking for help. A rottweiler called Sabre would not let his owner get back in his car, and things were getting desperate. When I arrived at the scene, Sabre was sitting in the back of the car looking very pleased with himself, but growling whenever the owner or the police tried to get him out. Using a catching pole, I was able to transfer Sabre from the car to my RSPCA van relatively easily, but I was concerned about how I was going to get him out once I got back to the shelter.

I was certain that by adopting a non-confrontational approach, I would be able to get Sabre to leave the van quietly. Over the years I had learned that a dog that is behaving aggressively will become even more aggressive if you attempt to invade its space. By the time we arrived back at the shelter Sabre appeared to be relaxed and happy. I opened the rear door of the van and he came up to me with his tail wagging and a friendly look on his face. He showed no sign at all of his previous aggression.

As it turned out, Sabre was car-protective. He hadn't been with his owner very long and had not had time to accept his owner's authority. The previous owner had trained Sabre to guard his car, and Sabre thought he was just doing his job.

Meter readers, postal workers and other door-to-door representatives

It may seem that people who regularly come into contact with dogs in the course of their work are less at risk of attack than a vet, for example, because they are not obliged to handle dogs. However, according to statistics, this is not the case. I believe that fear of the unknown is responsible for the high incidence of dog attacks in the service industry. Many of these people do not own a dog, are afraid of them, or simply do not like them. I also believe that the stories these workers pass on to each other add to the paranoia of some service industry and door-to-door representatives. During my research into the problems faced by these workers, I met with many people in the industry and found that the lunchroom talk mainly revolved around dogs.

Participants in these conversations appeared to be divided into three camps. There were those who knew nothing or very little about dogs, and they listened to anyone that they thought had the answers.

The second group had their own theories based on half-truths. They led the others to believe they have all the answers and convinced them that aggression is the only way to avoid attack, even though they themselves have been bitten on several occasions. The third group was less vocal, but had for years instinctively practised a technique identical to mine without realising that's why they were never bitten.

One of the main problems I have unearthed in the service industry is the widespread belief that aggression is the answer. This is partly due to lunchtime stories about how someone in the organisation has been able to scare off an aggressive dog by picking up a stick, a rock or kicking the dog. Because the dog in this case ran away, the technique appeared to be successful. However, a dog that runs away is not the type of dog that's likely to launch an attack. A dog with more courage that does not scare easily would not respond to an aggressive technique by fleeing – it would attack.

Safe property entry

Check to see if there is a dog on the property
Look for signs such as dirty marks on the verandah, caused by the oil from a dog's coat, which leaves a tell-tale sign on wood and fibro.

Entering gates
When entering a gate be aware that a dog could be lurking on the other side waiting for some unsuspecting person to stick their hand over the top of the gate to open it. If you rattle the gate, it will usually produce a bark from the dog, indicating to you that a dog is on the property and you need to be on your guard. Always study the dog's body language before entering the property.

Knocking on doors

Be aware that some people keep their dog inside the house, so you might not receive a warning bark. If there is a screen door, place your foot against the base of it to prevent a dog from accidentally springing the catch and being able to attack you.

Sandra, who worked for the Australian Electoral Commission, received the fright of her life when she knocked on a door one day. A large malamute came charging at her, as soon as the door was opened, crashing through the screen door and taking it off its hinges. Sandra landed flat on her back and the dog landed on top of her, the screen door firmly wedged between them. The dog just stood there licking her face.

If held in front of you, a large briefcase, a bag, a clipboard or a thick coat can protect you in an attack situation. Do not use it as a weapon – under no circumstances should you swing anything towards a charging dog.

Do not be aggressive

If you behave aggressively towards a dog you will only make the dog more aggressive. Even if the dog isn't aggressive towards you because you have it bluffed, it may show aggression towards your workmates. By behaving aggressively you are playing with dynamite. One day you will come across a dog that won't back down.

Do not believe the owner

Most dog owners have no concept of what their dog will do under certain circumstances. If you have to enter a property in the course of your work, politely ask the owner to confine their dog while you are there.

I recently had to have the battery changed on my car. When the mechanic arrived, he asked me to confine my dog while he worked on my car. Instinctively, I started to defend my dog and explain that he would not bite, but I stopped myself short, realising that I was not practising what I preached. The man went on to tell me that he had previously been attacked by a dog when he touched its owner's car. He knew first-hand how protective dogs can be of their owner's property.

There are several situations in which you could be bitten when on a property with both dog and owner. For instance, if shaking hands or handing something to the owner, the dog might view this as a threat to its owner and could attack. A dog and its owner equal a potentially dangerous combination, so always keep your eye on the dog's and the owner's movements.

When leaving a property, never turn your back on the dog. They often view leaving as a back-down and might just take the opportunity to give you a sneaky bite to send you on your way.

Case history

Des attended a property one day to disconnect the electricity supply because of an unpaid account. When he arrived, he was met by the owner and his bull terrier. The man said he had decided to pay the account and went inside to get a cheque. He returned a short time later, and as Des leaned towards him to accept the cheque, the dog leapt at Des, grabbing his arm.

Fortunately, Des did not recoil; he lowered his arm to the ground, going with the dog's movements as it landed back on its feet. The owner released the dog's grip and Des was unharmed.

Do not stare

Never, under any circumstances, should you stare at a dog. Staring will only incite it to attack if it's feeling uneasy about you. Dogs regard staring as a threatening and challenging act. Dominant dogs will stare at other dogs and submissive, non-challenging dogs will avert their eyes to avoid confrontation.

Maintain your height advantage

If you are sitting or kneeling down and a dog approaches, stand up immediately. Do not move until the dog has had a chance to assess you. If the dog attacks, follow the Stand Right No Bite™ technique.

Always carry food

I have found that people who use the food approach receive a very positive response from dogs. Many previously aggressive dogs are soon pacified once they are given something to eat.

It is best to carry dry food that fits easily into your pocket, such as dog biscuits or kibble. When the dog approaches you, throw some food on the ground. Do not attempt to pat the dog, but speak to it in a soft voice. You want it to recognise your voice and remember the food next time you visit.

Tips for bike riders

If you ride a motorcycle or pushbike to deliver the mail or papers, you are in a potentially more dangerous situation than anyone else. Can you imagine just what a dog sees? – a thing with two wheels, two legs that kick out at them, two arms and a head, definitely nothing like a human being.

The best way to prevent an attack in this situation is to always carry food. If a dog chases you, stop, get off the bike and remove your helmet. Stand up straight to assert your height dominance then throw some food on the ground for the dog. If it attacks you, use your bike to protect yourself.

Do not behave aggressively or try to kick the dog when you get back on the bike. It will only make the situation worse.

Using electronic devices

There are electronic devices that omit a high-frequency sound when activated. A few years ago these were hailed as the 'cure-all' of dog attacks. However, many service industries have now dispensed with them in favour of staff education.

One meter reader told me that on his first day at work he was given a kit, which contained a zapper. He said he felt like Billy the Kid. Whenever a dog came running, he'd activate the zapper and the dog would flee. He thought 'This is great, no dog will touch me'.

This approach worked well, until one day when he was reading a meter, a large dog came running round the corner, barking at him. He pointed the zapper at the dog and pressed the button. The dog kept coming. He threw the zapper at it and leapt over the fence.

In my experience, these devices only work on dogs that lack the confidence to attack anyway. Confident, aggressive dogs tend to become even more aggressive.

Remember, an aggressive approach is *always* dangerous, and only increases your chances of being attacked.

Author's note

The reasons why a dog will attack are numerous. In order to dispel the myths, avoid media hype and to prevent anxiety about certain breeds, I firmly believe there should be a dog control organisation in each state, responsible for investigating every attack a dog makes on a human. This would enable the collection and dissemination of accurate information as to why attacks occur. It would also assist law-makers to develop sensible legislation based on fact rather than supposition. As I write this, some members of parliament are proposing legislation that will make it a legal requirement for all dog owners to train their dogs. This, I feel, is a more realistic approach to dog control than banning certain breeds.

Keep in mind that humans hit with their hands and dogs with their teeth. When a person attacks another person, the attacker is brought to trial, all the facts are investigated and a reason behind the assault sought. Unfortunately, a dog that attacks a person is usually disposed of as quickly as possible and no defence is offered. If we knew the reasons behind each attack, we would be able to reduce their number.

Case history

I received a call from the police asking me to assess Bandit, an 18-month-old cattle dog accused of attacking three children while they were playing in a park. As a result of the attack, his owner Kelly was charged with owning a savage dog and was soon to appear in court. If she lost the case it would cost Bandit his life.

I rang Kelly and made an appointment to see Bandit the following day. She told me that he had attacked the children without provocation and with considerable frenzy. The children's mother had lifted them onto a slippery dip to keep them out of Bandit's reach. Kelly also said that her two teenage sons had been in charge of Bandit when he attacked, and that they didn't have him on a lead at the time.

When I first met Bandit he was behind a chainwire fence. He flew at the fence, growling, snapping and continually looking over his shoulder, displaying all the signs of a fearful dog.

I sat down with Kelly and asked her many questions. First, I wanted to know if she definitely wanted to keep him. I needed to know how seriously she would be committed to his rehabilitation. I also asked who normally walked him, if he had been given any formal training, and how much control she and her sons had over Bandit.

Kelly turned out to be a very devoted dog owner. She told me that Bandit had had no formal training. She loved him, wanted desperately to keep him, and would do everything I told her if it was going to save her dog's life. She also told me the boys were the only ones who walked Bandit and that they had very little control over him, as demonstrated on the day of the attack.

I asked Kelly to go into the backyard with Bandit while I approached the house from the street again. I wanted to see if I could show her how to gain greater control over him. That day, I was able to teach Kelly to communicate with her dog in a way that he could understand and to get the message through to him that she did not approve of his aggression.

I filled out my report to the police the next day. In part, it read as follows:

'It is my belief that Bandit is of a fearful nature and that his fear was possibly aggravated by the inexperience of the children in charge of him. I suggest that in order to prevent an occurrence of the same problem, the following procedures must be adhered to:

Bandit should receive extensive obedience training from Bark Busters™.
No person under 18 years of age should walk or be placed in charge of Bandit outside his property.
The dog in question should at all times be walked on lead and should be muzzled when outside the property.
Any form of aggression by Bandit should be met with disapproval by his owners.'

I recommended that I be asked to do a follow-up assessment in six weeks' time.

At her court appearance one week later, Kelly was fined $400 and instructed to abide by the recommendations in my report.

When I reassessed Bandit six weeks later, I was elated by his improvement. He was no longer displaying the signs of a fearful dog; instead, he was relaxed and friendly, even allowing me to pat him. As long as Kelly kept him under strict control and maintained the training, I knew Bandit would be unlikely to attack someone ever again.

Some five years on I ran into Kelly while out shopping. She stopped me in the street, asking me if I remembered her. She told me that she still had Bandit and that he had never bitten anyone again since the training Bark Busters™ gave her. She acknowledged that it was her inexperience and lack of knowledge that caused Bandit's aggression in the first place.

As this case history shows, it is possible to rehabilitate an aggressive dog. I am aware that some readers may be horrified that I am advocating such a radical approach, but experience has taught me that a dog with a history of aggressive behaviour can be rehabilitated if the owner is totally committed to maintaining strict control and training. The onus always lies with the dog's owner – no dog can be held accountable for its actions. Remember, dogs are pets, and by choosing to own a dog, we have to accept responsibility for its behaviour.

13

Dealing with an over-excitable dog

The most common cause of excitability in dogs is an unbalanced diet. Some dogs appear to overreact to certain colourings, preservatives or grains present in some pre-prepared foods.

At Bark Busters™ we have discovered that by altering the diet of excitable dogs, we are able to calm them down dramatically. By replacing a diet that is full of preservatives, colourings or high in grain, with a diet void of colourings, preservatives and that is low in carbohydrates, a transformation can be achieved almost overnight.

The problems associated with food colourings and preservatives are well documented when it comes to causing hyperactivity in children. However, at Bark Busters™ we have found that dogs are just as sensitive to these ingredients.

Excessive amounts of grain in a dog's diet may make a dog behave hyperactively. Significant changes take place once grains are removed from the diet of hyperactive dogs.

The idea that excessive amounts of grain in the diet might be the cause of hyperactivity in dogs sent to us for treatment occurred to me one day when I was feeding my horse. I had been away travelling for a week and had asked a friend to feed my horse in my absence. When I fed him on my return, this wild, but normally placid animal was now rearing up in the air near his feed bowl.

I could hardly believe my eyes. I immediately rang my friend to find out what she had been feeding him that was different from his normal diet. She told me that she had decided to give him a treat of a mixture of grains.

The following case histories are designed to highlight how the wrong diet can be instrumental in creating hyperactivity in some dogs.

Case history

A Bark Busters™ therapist was called in to assess Bozo, a Jack Russell terrier. The therapist was astounded by the way Bozo greeted her. He leapt and jumped on every piece of furniture in the house, across benchtops, then leapt about at her feet, barking and spinning. When the therapist arrived, he was running around, carrying a knife in his mouth.

His owners, Matthew and Joanne, were at their wits' end. They told the therapist that this was the way Bozo behaved all day long. They had tried everything, including training with food, using a water squirter and many types of training methods, all without success.

Several dog trainers had already beaten a path to their door, but each time went away scratching their heads. The therapist asked about Bozo's diet and was led to the pantry. She noted that his diet was a 'high performance' dry food biscuit.

The therapist arranged to return in three days' time, meanwhile suggesting that Bozo's diet be changed from the high performance biscuit to a diet low in carbohydrates, free from colourings and preservatives, in an effort to calm him down. A diet rich in mutrients from raw, meaty bones and raw food was suggested.

The therapist returned three days later. The change in Bozo was so significant that the therapist thought at first that Matthew and Joanne had bought another dog.

Bozo was much calmer, he was no longer like a wound-up spring. He was still full of life, but definitely much more controllable.

Case history

Casper, a 12-month-old Japanese spitz, was creating many problems for his elderly owner, Harold. Harold was finding it difficult to sleep at night, as Casper did not appear to want to sleep, but just barked most of the night.

Harold called Bark Busters™, and a therapist attended. Treatment was commenced to show Harold how to assert his dominance, using body language and guttural correction (the 'Bah' word and clapping).

The therapist inquired as to the diet Casper was being fed and was told it was colour and preservative free.

Casper's first session proved very successful, and a second lesson was scheduled for a week later.

Three days later Harold rang the therapist. Casper was much better but was still not sleeping at night, and he was barking most of the night. Harold was spending most of the night getting out of his bed to correct Casper's barking.

The therapist returned the next day, this time requesting to look at the label of the food that Casper was eating. It was labelled 'High performance'. The therapist suggested that Casper should be fed a diet that was naturally low in carbohydrates.

Harold rang two days later to say that he had just had his first full night's sleep in six months.

As detailed in the following case history, excitement in dogs isn't always diet related, but can sometimes be due to its breeding. Discipline coupled with the right diet is the best way to solve over-excitement problems.

Case history

Bark Busters™ was initially contacted to treat Rocky, a miniature pinscher, for aggression towards other dogs. His owner, Glenda, had ceased walking him, because she feared confrontations with other dogs due to his anti-social behaviour.

We soon realised that Rocky was definitely not behaving in an aggressive way but rather in an excitable way. He would become very excited each time he sighted a dog off in the distance while on his walk. His excitement would grow the nearer the dog came.

We first suggested that a Halti be fitted to assist Glenda to control his excitement, as she was a very soft-natured lady with an almost inaudible voice. (A halti is halter-like head coller, much like a horse halter, that fits over the dog's head. As the halti is fixed to the head, it prevents the dog from being able to pull to the same degree that it can with its neck muscles, making it easier to handle a strong, bolsterous dog.) She needed to show Rocky that she was the boss. We also suggested that he be walked on a loose lead, as this was the reason he had become so excited in the first place.

Once the Halti was fitted, Glenda was instructed to ensure that the lead was not pulled tight but always remained loose. She was shown how to correct his behaviour with the 'Bah' and the clap when Rocky was thinking of becoming excited, which was when he first spotted the dogs, not once the adrenaline was already pumping. He then calmly walked past several dogs without any adverse reaction whatsoever.

Excitement manifests itself in many ways. It can be the dog that bounds all over the house, the dog that barks all night or the one that barks each time it sees another dog. The dog may be on the wrong diet, or it might be due to the dogs' breeding or lack of proper leadership. At Bark Busters™ we recommend that owners research the right diet for their dog's needs.

Dogs that are easily excited need calm owners who are in control. The calmer you are, the better. You also need to be calm and in control of your feelings before attempting to quell the excitement of an excitable dog. Dogs are very intuitive. Whenever I have seen an excitable dog, I have seen an equally excitable owner. Dogs will become more frenzied in their behaviour if the owner appears to have lost control of the situation.

Summary:

- Check your dog's diet: is it high in carbohydrates, preservatives or colouring?
- Excitable dogs need strong leaders.
- Be calm and in control when your dog is behaving in an excitable way.

14

Dogs and children

Never leave a baby or child alone with any dog. In the wild mother dogs are very protective of their puppies, never allowing any other dogs in the pack to approach them while they are young. It is not unusual for a dog to perceive a puppy, especially those of the same sex, as a future threat to their position within the pack. This can apply even when the pack members are human.

A lady in the United States was visiting with her friend who owned six chihuahuas. During the visit the lady left her baby on the lounge while she and her friend left the room. The mother returned a few minutes later to find that the dogs had killed her baby. No mother dog would never leave her puppies alone in that situation – instinct would have warned her of the dangers. Perhaps the dogs' owner even assured her that the dogs posed no threat. Perhaps their size supported that impression.

rate your dog's behavior at www.barkbusters.com

Although what happened was horrendous, I don't think that the dogs intended to kill the baby. It is more likely that they were asserting their dominance. However, the victim was a tiny, helpless baby. It would not have taken long before the poor baby succumbed to its injuries.

No matter how much you trust your dog you cannot predict what will happen if you leave it alone with a child. Your child might do something that incites or upsets the dog. Attacks on children are very common, with many children suffering horrendous injuries. This could be avoided if children and dogs were always monitored when together.

Of course I am not suggesting that all domestic dogs will attack a child if given the chance. The risk of this happening is really very small, but any risk where a baby or young child is concerned is a risk no parent should take.

Never allow a dog to snatch food from your child

A female dog in the wild would never allow another dog to take food from her offspring; she would attack and repel any dog that attempted such a thing. This would soon be common knowledge among the pack members. They would soon learn to stay clear of the puppies when they were eating as they have their mother nearby to protect them.

By correcting your dog when it tries to take food off your child you are actually establishing them as a protected species. In the dog's eyes they are 'the untouchables'.

When you discipline your dog for this behaviour, you are imitating the way the female dog would protect her babies. Your actions teach your dog that your child must be respected. The dog will soon learn that your child/children have the same status as you.

Be aware that children will naturally want to emulate their parents, but must be carefully instructed not to copy the adult's lead. One way to ensure this rule is obeyed is to always ensure that the adults in the family monitor the children when they are with the dog.

Walking in and out of doors

To make certain that your dog has a continuing respect for your child, you must ensure that it never dominates the child. By this I mean when entering a door or moving from room to room, you must ensure that all members of the family, including any children enter a room before the

dog. If the dog pushes past your child knocking it over, then correct it verbally, clap your hands, use a water squirter or use your Bark Busters™ pillow (available from your nearest Bark Busters™ office, with a lesson) to let it know that the behaviour is totally unacceptable.

Children under 12 years of age should never correct or reprimand any dog.

Case history

John and Marie took their little Jack Russell, Jack, to the vets to be put to sleep. He had just bitten their eight-year-old son Michael on the face, missing his eye by centimetres. The whole family was devastated because they loved Jack so much. He was part of the family, but Michael could have lost his eye, and they did not want to take the chance that it might happen again.

The vet suggested that they give Bark Busters™ a call.

One of our country therapists was called in to attend, and as I happened to be in town, I went along.

John and Marie relayed the story of how Michael came to be attacked by Jack. It had happened early one morning while John and Marie were still in bed. Michael had called out to tell his parents that Jack was on the lounge again. They called back telling Michael to get him off. Then Michael screamed in pain because Jack had just bitten him.

We prodded them for some more information.

Had Jack ever bitten anyone before?

Had he ever growled at anyone in the family?

Was he obedient?

Did he have any behavioural problems?

They told us that Jack had never bitten anyone before and he'd never growled. However he was not obedient and had several problems. He would never go outside when told, he would jump on the lounge, refuse to get off, he would bark at the neighbours and refuse to listen to anyone.

It was obvious that Jack had little respect for anyone in the family and we were amazed that something like this attack, or at least a warning, had never happened before.

We explained to John and Marie that Michael was not of an age where he should be allowed to discipline Jack and that we believed this to be one of the reasons he was bitten. We also discovered through more questioning and prodding that Jack did not like anyone touching his collar. He would growl at them and try to bite their hands. This was the method the whole family had used to get him off the lounge or to put him outside, as he would not go willingly.

This revelation was no surprise to us, as we were accustomed to people not making the connection between aggression in one area being related to an attack in another situation.

We knew that Jack's dislike for having his collar touched was the main source of the problem. They had totally overlooked his behaviour, when trying to touch his collar, not realising it was related to the reason Michael was attacked. Another strange thing, but one that was not new to us, was that they had not considered the growling and snapping at their hands when they tried to grab his collar as a form of aggression.

We explained that the reason the problem occurred in the first place was related to the fact that the whole family was dealing with the problems they had with Jack in a physical way. When Jack would not go outside or refused to get off the lounge, everyone in the family would take turns at grabbing his collar and making him do it.

We assured them that we would show them how to get Jack to respond to a command and go outside willingly without any use of physical force.

To some people this form of physical control is quite normal. If a child is on a lounge and they are asked to get off but refuse, the next logical step might be to take them by the arm and physically move them off.

Dogs do not respond well to any form of physical force. They are driven by the flight or fight response when they are restrained physically. If they cannot flee, their response will nearly always be to bite. They also soon learn that if you bite the hand it releases its grip. This, of course, is not the case with all dogs. Many dogs will allow their owners to lead them by the collar.

We also explained to John and Marie that another reason for the attack on Michael was his age. As he had no pack status in Jack's eyes, he was reprimanded for his insolence. The attack occurred because Jack was already in the habit of biting any hand that tried to get hold of his collar. This had not worked for him as well as he expected because he would still be dragged outside. So he escalated the aggression to the next level by biting at Michael's face in order to stop him from grabbing the collar. He had leapt at Michael in an effort to stop Michael (a subordinate) from grabbing his collar and dragging him off the lounge.

We also explained that we believed that if John and Marie had been in the same room as Michael that Jack might never have attacked in this way. He would have been aware that Michael would have had backup from the adults who had slightly more authority and he would have been reluctant to incur their wrath.

Attacks like the one discussed above are commonplace. The problem starts out as a minor one, with the dog controlling the family with snaps and growls. Then one day a child in the family tries to emulate what the adults have been doing, or tries to get the dog to do something that it does when the adults are present, and the dog launches an attack. The dog does not view the child as having any authority and with the absence of the adults doesn't think twice about disciplining the child.

Tips for parents

Statistics show that children are more likely to be attacked by a dog they know, either their own or that of a friend.

As a parent it is your responsibility to do all within your power to prevent your child from being attacked by a dog. The following advice will help you to keep your child safe:

Summary:

- Never leave a child alone with any dog.
- When visiting friends who have a dog, do not allow your child to play in the yard near the dog unsupervised. If that's not possible, ask the owners to confine the dog away from the child.
- Do not allow your child to feed any dog. Instead, do it yourself and allow them to assist.
- Do not allow your child to pull at a dog in order to get it to do something – teach the dog to respond to a verbal command.
- By law children under 18 years of age should never walk a dog without adult supervision as the dog could drag them unwittingly into a fight.
- Never give your child a dog as a toy substitute – a dog is a living creature that has feelings. Children should be taught from an early age to respect a dog's feelings.

15

Communicating with your dog

Using the dog's language to communicate effectively

If we want to communicate with dogs effectively, we need to employ the language they use to communicate. Dogs cannot understand our language, but can learn to recognise the sounds of the words uttered or key phrases, if they are kept simple. You could liken this to the way you would communicate with someone who is only just learning to speak your language. You would communicate with simple, short phrases rather than long sentences.

A dog's brain works very similarly to a computer. It remembers everything that it processes and when the right buttons are pushed, will respond with the correct response.

They do not lie around thinking about things the way that humans do, for example, whether it's going to rain, whether the electricity bill has been paid or if there is enough food in the fridge. They *will* think about rain when the signs are evident. It is then that their computer-like brain receives the information. They will think about food when they are hungry but will never consider the electricity. Dogs are only interested in knowing what they need to know.

Communicating using the dog's method

To be able to communicate with your dog you must emulate the way dogs relay messages to each other. This means using similar body language coupled with guttural sounds.

For many years now I have closely studied the way dogs communicate with each other. It has taught me to be able to read their every thought. I can now predict what they will do well before they do it. Owners are constantly astounded at my accurate predictions about how their dog will behave. They imagine that I'm some kind of clairvoyant. However, I just have a very clear understanding of the dog's every gesture, reading their language quickly and effectively, consequently being able to predict their next move.

Understanding how a dog communicates is very important when it comes to training and resolving its everyday behavioural problems. Communication between human and dog is the most important part of any training regime and the main tool to successfully being able to train your puppy. Without a communication link between you and your dog, you will not progress very far. You will endure endless frustrating hours of yelling and screaming, resulting in either total confusion from your puppy or no response whatsoever.

You will begin to think you are speaking in an alien tongue and you will be right. Human language means nothing to a dog. It's only through time and continuous banter that a dog begins to learn what certain words mean. They will learn those words involved with food and going for a walk long before they will learn the other less interesting words such as 'come' or 'sit'.

These sounds are not as interesting or as important to the dog as those sounds that the dog perceives to be related to its survival.

So how do we, a sophisticated, highly evolved species, establish a communication link with the dog, a creature that has a very primitive language? It stands to reason that we must take our level of communication down to the dog's level if we want the dog to understand what we are saying.

Dogs do not use sophisticated speech to relay messages to other canines. Instead they use body language and guttural sounds to get their message through to each other. Their body gestures, positions and movement can say so many things.

The dog's body language

To let other dogs know what they are thinking and feeling a dog uses the language of body movements, gestures and positions. They will stand tall, with tail and ears held high to relay feelings of confidence and dominance to other dogs.

On the other hand, a dog that is feeling inferior or wishes to relay to the opposing dog a message of 'I'm no threat to you' will lower its height and make its ears lie flat against its head. It might even roll over, placing itself in a very vulnerable position and exposing its neck and throat. This is the equivalent to an army laying down its weapons. They are showing that they no longer pose a threat to their opponents.

In the dog's eyes, body height plays a significant role in determining hierarchy. It doesn't really matter if the two dogs are of different height, it really has more to do with how they carry themselves, and how they use the height that they have. I have seen a chihuahua dominating a German shepherd. The size of the dog isn't relevant to determining pack order. You could say it's not the size of the dog in the fight, but the size of the fight in the dog that counts.

Humans have similar gestures to display dominance. We all know when we have met someone very dominant. We think 'I don't feel comfortable in that person's company.'

Because dogs don't possess the complicated language we do, they have evolved into the world's greatest body language readers, interpreting everything we do, trying in their way to understand what we are saying.

People consider life most often in terms of 'they said this or they said that', 'did you hear what he said?' and so on. We tend not to say, 'Did you see the way he lowered his head when he said that?' or 'Did you see the way he gestured with his right hand when he said goodbye?'.

The dog communicates its every thought through its body language. It uses audible guttural tones such as growling to communicate dissatisfaction. It uses barking as a way of warding off intruders into its territory or as a way of rallying other pack members.

To the trained eye the dog's every move communicates exactly what it's feeling, what it is about to do and whether it's frightened, vulnerable, confident or hesitant.

Dogs are also avid observers of other dogs' body language as well as human body language. Dogs have no concept that we are a different species. More than likely dogs think that people are also dogs that walk on two legs – the tallest dogs in the world.

Dogs instinctively know the meaning of any gesture another dog makes. A dog that is stiff and rigid is ready for action, sizing up the situation first, and making its assessment of the other dog before going into battle or moving on. A dog that is staring at another dog with the same stillness is challenging the other dog and on the verge of an attack. Dogs need to understand these body poses that each other makes so they can act accordingly.

If a person emulated any of these body actions they could be sending the dog the wrong message without realising it. For example, staring at a dog that is of a dominant nature could easily provoke an attack because staring tells the dog 'I am going to attack you'. A dominant dog would be more likely to leap into action and attack rather than back down like a submissive dog.

On the other hand, if we are crouching or sitting down we are telling the dog that we are a pushover because we are displaying the body language of a submissive dog. A more dominant dog might try to dominate a person when they view them as being subservient.

Case history

Many years ago when I first began to learn the significance of dogs' body language, I was lying down outside enjoying a peaceful time by the pool with my beloved, very obedient German shepherd, Monty. He kept pestering me, licking my face and generally making a nuisance of himself. I growled the 'Bah' correction word which he always obeyed, but he simply ignored it and continued to annoy me.

I had never known him to disobey me in this way before. I growled again but it was as if I had said nothing as Monty didn't bat an eyelid. I was now becoming very frustrated and a little annoyed. I rose up onto my elbows and he just kept licking me, I stood up to my full height and noticed a huge change in his demeanour. He immediately became more compliant. I growled, and he went to find a spot on the grass to lie down. I returned to my spot to lie down and as I did so Monty rose again and headed for me. I jumped up again and growled, and he lay down.

I had been given my first lesson in the language of the dog. If you show submissive body language, the dog will dominate you, but if you show dominant body language, the dog will submit.

A dog's guttural language

Dogs will bark to summon the rest of the pack whether the pack is made up of humans or other dogs. Dogs understand instinctively that they rely heavily on the other members of the pack and need the numbers to repel an attack. When a threat is discovered, they will bark frantically. Even a solitary dog will still instinctively carry out this ritual barking to call the pack while endeavouring to chase away the intruder.

Dogs will use the growl tones of their vocabulary generally to relay displeasure with what is happening at the time or if they feel threatened. This growl is used as a warning. In dogs' language it means, 'Keep doing what you are doing and I will bite you'. No self-respecting dog that has no wish for trouble would continue to proceed after hearing this sound. In dog language it's a red light. It means stop, do not proceed.

Dogs also use a chattering, whining high-pitched sound that indicates happiness, excitement or frustration. This is generally used to get the pack's attention quickly, but without the urgency or warning sound of the bark. Most dogs will willingly come to investigate this sound. You can mimic this chattering sound by using a quick succession of 'pup pup pup' sounds uttered in a very high-pitched tone, coupled with quick, soft, successive claps. Most dogs come running when they hear these sounds.

The howling sound, quite often used by malamutes, huskies and the like, is not commonly used by domestic dogs, although it can be triggered by the sound of another dog howling or when fire engines or ambulances (which closely mimic the sound) are heard. Dogs that hear these sounds have to howl. They cannot stop themselves, in much the same way that people yawn when someone else does.

Using a dog's language to communicate effectively

Now that you know the way that dogs communicate, it stands to reason if we employ the same technique that dogs use, we can relay our messages to the dog instantly.

First we must employ the same body language or as close as practicable to the way dogs relay messages to each other. For example, if we want to relay strength or dominance, then we must stand tall when requesting our dog to obey. If we want our dog to approach us willingly, we must lower our height to entice our dog to approach, then regain it when our dog approaches.

It is very difficult for a dog to approach another dog, which it views us to be, if the other dog is standing in a dominant pose. The lowering of height should only be until such time as the dog has approached and feels welcomed, then the height can be regained.

If we are unhappy with our dog's behaviour, then we must mimic the way dogs relay disapproval by growling our disapproval and adopting dominant body language, i.e. standing erect. This should then be followed by 'good boy', uttered in a high-pitched tone to excite the dog when we are happy with it.

The words you use with your dog are superfluous, as your dog will only react to the sound of the word, not what you are saying. You could be saying, 'You are a naughty little boy and I'm going to smack your bottom' but because you are saying it in a high-pitched voice, your dog will react favourably.

You could also say 'Good dog' in a guttural tone, mimicking the growl tone, and your dog would think that you are displeased with it.

I gained this knowledge over many years of studying and observing the behaviour of dogs. Being able to read their every thought is now a gift I treasure very much, one that has helped me immensely with my everyday work. It means I am able to help others gain this insight.

You too can achieve great results with your dog by using the dogs' system of communication.

If we were to focus away from the speech that humans use, to their natural body gestures, we would very soon begin to notice that there are many parallels between the gestures that humans make and those that dogs make. Humans could silently communicate with each other in a primitive language if we chose to. People do use body language and we can read it – sometimes we just don't realise that we can. People stand tall when confronted by any opposition, when discussions become heated it is commonplace to see people begin to stand up. People will go for height to make them feel superior by either sitting on a higher chair or stool or when a teacher stands at the head of the class. These are all human actions that make us appear more dominant and in control.

Our words can mask our actions. We can say, 'It's nice to meet you' and smile while we really mean, 'What are you doing here?' A dog's words never mask its actions. Its growl is clear and concise. It is saying, 'Stop doing what you are doing.' There is no mistaking that.

People who are feeling vulnerable and lack confidence will generally lower their demeanour, sit down, and hunch up their shoulders. More subordinate people will move out of the way of more dominant people.

I see people behaving in exactly this way with their dog, thinking it's a simple creature and that none of their actions have any significance. They step aside to allow the dog to walk past them or allow the dog to dominate them by jumping on them, and then pat it for doing so.

If you want to be in control of your dog, you must always appear to be the dominant partner in the relationship. Use the dog's set of body movements to your advantage. Stand your ground, do not move around your dog when it blocks your way, but make it move out of your way. It is testing you for dominance.

Stand tall and erect when correcting any undesirable behaviour, and don't chase after your dog, but make it come to you.

Understanding your dog's body language

When learning to communicate effectively with your dog you must emulate or copy the way a dog would communicate with other dogs.

A dog uses certain body movements and gestures to relay messages to other canines. A dog that is standing tall and rigid with its tail and ears forward is relaying strength of character, confidence and dominance.

A dog displaying dominance would almost be on 'tiptoe'. It would be standing tall and erect, taking very definite steps with very little body movement. If the other dog leapt or jumped on the dominant dog, the dominant dog would more than likely freeze the action and stand its ground in an effort to relay its displeasure. If the other dog continued to take liberties, the dominant dog would then growl. If the other dog also ignored this growl, then the dominant dog would more than likely snap at the offending dog. If this was also ignored, the dominant dog's usual course of action is to take the proceedings to the final level, which would be to fight. This scenario is usually where two dogs of equal dominance meet and the second dog refuses to submit.

At the other end of the scale, a dog that is lowering its height, tail and ears is indicating to the other dog that it is no threat and definitely not attempting to challenge the other dog's authority.

Likewise when you want your dog to obey your command and you display body language similar to that of a subordinate dog, your dog will not view you as being authoritative enough to be able to back up your convictions. Most probably it will simply ignore you. Even though you might be growling at your dog, if you are displaying submissive body language, it will more than likely view the growling as fear rather than a display of dominance.

Voice tones

We can emulate the way a dog communicates by coupling the exact type of body language with the correct vocal tone, using certain voice tones. If we are displeased with our puppy then we can communicate our displeasure by growling while standing up to our full height. This is the exact way your dog's mother would have let it know that she is displeased with its behaviour.

If we are pleased, we will lift our voice up a few octaves to an excited chatter and high-pitched tone, saying 'Good puppy, good boy'. This high-pitched tone has a way of exciting the pup and is very similar to the sound dogs make when they are excited.

An excited puppy will make a yap! yap! yap! high-pitched sound when its mother approaches or when it becomes excited about an impending event. By using this tone when your puppy pleases you, you encourage it to repeat the good behaviour in the future.

Case study

Judy, the owner of a silky terrier named Pixie, was having problems getting her dog to come when it was called. Judy would try everything within her power to get Pixie to come to her but Pixie would just stand there looking at her and refuse to come to her.

Judy had tried all of the common methods such as offering food, running in the opposite direction, and crouching down, but still Pixie refused to come anywhere near her. Judy called Bark Busters™ for assistance. Judy showed me what she was doing with Pixie and how she was calling her. I noticed Judy's voice tones were very harsh, both when she called Pixie and when she praised her.

I suggested that she change her voice tone from the harsh one she was using to a lighter tone. I pointed out that the harsh tones she was using to call Pixie were actually a reprimand, and that was why Pixie was just standing looking at her. She was afraid to approach her growling owner.

Judy took my advice and changed her tone, Pixie ran to her immediately with her tail wagging.

Praise

Praise is one of the most important communication tools. When praising you must ensure that the praise follows immediately after the cessation of the bad behaviour. Do not carry a correction on longer than is necessary.

If you pat your puppy while delivering praise, you will instil in your puppy that 'good dog' means something pleasurable is about to happen. This way your puppy is more likely to want to stop the bad behaviour and will seek out the praise.

Praise can also be used to reassure a puppy that is unsure if it has done the right thing for those puppies that are lacking confidence. Some people focus so much on making their puppies do the right thing, that they forget to praise and their puppy stands there frozen to the spot, afraid to make a move for fear of doing the wrong thing again.

If you keep your communication clear and precise and remember to praise the instant your puppy stops the bad behaviour, your puppy will catch on quicker and stop its bad behaviour in no time.

The correct guttural word

The first thing you need is a word that lets your dog know it has made a mistake. The word I use is 'Bah'. If used gutturally, the way a dog would growl, it will work very effectively.

The 'Bah' word is not a magic word. If used normally without any guttural inference the chances are your dog will completely ignore it. Yet if it is used correctly in a growl tone, your dog should react to it and respond quickly.

The correct tones

When training your dog there are three distinct voice tones you will need to employ.

They are as follows:

- Low voice tone and growl 'Bah' for anything your dog does wrong.
- High-pitched voice tone and say 'Good dog' for when your dog responds to the growl.
- Normal voice tone for those times when you need to command your dog. Such as 'Come!' and 'Sit!' and so on.

The correct body language

In order to be your dog's leader and have it respond to your requests, you must at all times display the correct body language. I see many situations where dogs ignore an owner's request simply because the owner is sitting down. As soon as I tell them to stand up to their full height, their dog responds immediately.

Why do dogs react in this way? As mentioned, body language is the dog's predominant language, so the sounds they make are secondary to their body language.

When correcting your dog's undesirable behaviour you must deliver your corrections using the same language a dominant dog would use. Stand tall and stand your ground, growl the 'Bah' word, use the clap (the dog's equivalent of the snap if required), then praise all desired results.

If you initially remain seated when your dog is misbehaving then more than likely you will find your dog will ignore you because you are emulating the language of a subordinate dog. When relaying messages to your dog, use their language not yours.

Summary:

- When communicating with your dog, use its language.
- Stand tall, remain still and growl when correcting undesirable behaviour.
- Praise your dog the instant it responds favourably.

Education

Dogs learn by association. This simply means that if they experience something such as getting their tail slammed in a red door, then when the exact same set of circumstances arise again the dog will remember the previous time. The same dog might go through several yellow doors and not have a fear but will refuse to enter the red one again, fearing that the same thing will happen.

On the other hand, some dogs may refuse to enter any coloured door ever again. Even though the dog may have entered the red door several times prior to the tail-jamming incident, the dog still remembers the one bad experience and then commits that to memory as something it will never do again.

So when training your dog you must try to ensure that only good experiences occur if you don't want a puppy that is frightened of certain things.

When I take a young dog out in public for the first time, I am very diligent about everything I do and where I go with my young charge. I take the job of educating a young dog very seriously, keeping a very close eye on all proceedings to ensure that no mishaps occur that might scar a very young and impressionable mind. I watch out for people who might inadvertently step on its tail while we are in town. I keep a look out for dogs that are running free who might take a snap. I do my utmost to ensure that we only have positive experiences.

Case history

Tonka, a magnificent pure-bred German shepherd, was taken at the age of eight weeks to a puppy school that used very forceful methods for training puppies to walk on the lead. The puppies were yanked through the air on lead when they pulled in the wrong direction.

When I finally met Tonka he was eight months old and had a severe tail-chasing problem, which we had been called in to treat. However, although the tail chasing was chronic, the way that Tonka walked when on the lead concerned me and prompted me to ask his owners some more questions. He walked like a crouched tiger, half crawling and half walking, almost as if he was waiting for something bad to happen to him. When his owners revealed the technique they had been trained to use, the reason for his strange walk became crystal clear.

He was afraid of being yanked through the air, and although his owners had long since ceased using this technique, it was firmly implanted in Tonka's mind and only proper re-educating was going to remove it.

We spent a week retraining him, reassuring him that the bad stuff was a thing of the past. He now walks normally and very happily wherever his owners want to take him.

Although Tonka's owners had not used the yanking technique for many months, he still associated the lead as a tool of horror and acted accordingly. This is how the association factor works. When dogs experience a particular thing once and the same set of circumstances becomes evident in the future, they will always expect that that same event is going to recur.

The necessity for both adult members of the family to work to enable them to pay their mortgage leaves the family dog to its own devices for long hours at a time. It's this solitary confinement that creates many of the behavioural problems we are now seeing in dogs. Another contributing factor is the new wave of dog-training methods presently sweeping the world that do not focus on the dog's need for a leader.

Many of these techniques are based primarily on the premise of only offering positive responses for good behaviour and completely ignoring bad behaviour. This technique does not work on the stronger temperament dog that is about to do something wrong and cannot be stopped if its owner has no 'stop' mechanism.

Although positive training does work on many dogs and it sits better with dog owners who like the positive approach to training, it does not work with the strong, determined temperaments, largely because the owner has no form of discipline to stop the behaviour. It also goes against the dog's law.

People are horrified when their dogs react out of character like Zorro in the case history on 'tips for expectant parents'. The same people fail to realise that this is the dogs' natural way. Humans have made changes through domestication, but the 'wild dog' is always sitting there simmering below the surface.

I believe it's this lack of leadership in many of the modern training methods that is one of the main reasons we are experiencing more incidents of dog attacks. Dogs need leadership to feel safe in their environment or they will become neurotic, destructive and aggressive. Without strong leadership, dogs become delinquent and totally uncontrollable.

16

Dealing with barking

Barking is considered to be one of the most difficult canine problems to cure as well as being rated as the most annoying behavioural problem a dog can have. I believe the reason people consider it to be the most difficult to cure is because they tend to go about solving the problem in precisely the wrong way.

At Bark Busters™ we specialise in curing what is referred to as 'nuisance barking'. This is where a dog barks unnecessarily at things around its territory.

Barking is a very emotive issue. Dog owners want their dogs to bark to warn them of approaching danger. Neighbours or non-dog owners want peace and quiet. Councils have the right to police the *Dog Act*. Complaints received about barking dogs amount to the greatest number of complaints to local councils.

We have discovered that by working on curing nuisance barking we are able to appease all parties concerned. The neighbours are happy because the barking is dramatically reduced. The councils are happy because the neighbours are no longer complaining and the dog owner is happy because they still have an early warning system.

Because of their ability to learn by association, dogs can soon learn, with training, to bark only at those things that pose a threat to their territory not the everyday events that pose no threat, such as the neighbours moving about in their own yard, the neighbours' dog, cats, birds that fly into your yard, or passersby. The dog has to learn to coexist with these everyday occurrences.

Why dogs bark

Dogs use barking as a way of calling for the pack. If a dog is in the backyard barking at the next-door neighbour and the dog's owner runs outside yelling and screaming, then the dog has achieved its aim.

Considering the above scenario in the way a dog would helps us to understand why barking is deemed a difficult problem to cure. The dog is calling for the pack, the pack appears and they bark in their own fashion, which means the dog has achieved what it set out to achieve.

Another common thing owners do when attempting to cure barking is they tend to give the dog a command, rather than a correction. For example, the dog runs at the fence barking. The owner runs outside and says, 'Go and lie down!'. The dog obeys. The problem is that the dog doesn't think it has been corrected for its behaviour. Instead it has been given a command, which it has obeyed.

A similar scenario for humans would be me walking towards a hole in the ground that is obscured by long grass. My friend knows the hole is there and wants to warn me about it. There are two ways they can stop me: one way is to give me a command and say, 'Sylvia, come over here and sit down!'. If I'm obedient, more than likely I will turn around and sit down as requested. However, there is nothing to stop me from repeating the same mistake again, especially if they go away and leave me to my own devices. The second way they can stop me from stepping into the hole is by correcting my behaviour by saying, 'Sylvia, no!' This second approach immediately lets me know that I am about to make a mistake. I have received the message loud and clear.

Other people when trying to solve their dog's barking problems will either reward the dog by bringing it inside or punish it by hitting it when it approaches them or locking it up. All of these methods will fail miserably. Dogs learn by association. If they are barking and receive a call to go inside they will very soon learn that if they want to go inside all they need to do is bark.

The dog that is locked up or hit will only associate going to their owner as the reason for the punishment. It will not associate the barking as being the reason for the punishment.

Barking out of fear

Dogs use guttural sounds to relay messages to other dogs. Growling is generally used as a message of disapproval or when the dog is feeling vulnerable and frightened, perceiving that it is in danger.

Barking is a way of warding off interlopers to the dog's territory and rallying the rest of the pack. Fearful dogs that are left alone in a yard or house will generally bark more than confident dogs. Their fear escalates because they are frantically calling for the pack to rally and assist them to ward off the intruders or the perceived danger. If the pack fails to rally, they will become even more frantic. They do not feel that they are strong enough leaders to cope with any intruders to the territory and will therefore bark at the slightest noise or movement, worried that someone is approaching that they will very soon have to deal with and repel.

Their attempts to ward off the danger will become more frantic the nearer the danger approaches.

Case history

Sergeant, a two-year-old schnauzer who lived at a winery, was driving his owners Shirley and Jim to distraction with his frantic barking. They called in Bark Busters™ to treat his problem. I took one of my trainee therapists along for the experience.

We arrived to find Sergeant standing at the gate, frothing at the mouth while he frantically barked at us.

We sat down with Shirley and Jim in a quiet spot away from Sergeant's din and began explaining the reasons for his barking. We explained that his barking was a result of his fear of strangers and a lack of leadership. We explained the 'lone soldier' scenario to them and laughed at the significance of his name 'Sergeant', saying his personality is really more in keeping with that of a 'Private'.

Shirley and Jim caught on immediately, so we explained how to solve it. Shirley and Jim had to show Sergeant that he did not need to concern himself with warding off visitors to the property as he was now going to have, with our assistance, very strong leaders.

I pointed out to them that when they began correcting his barking using the Bark Busters™ technique he would no doubt run and hide. I explained that this would occur because of Sergeant's fearful nature.

When they stopped him barking (which he considered to be his weapon for warding off intruders), it would be the equivalent of taking the gun away from the lone soldier. Without a gun, when faced with the enemy, the soldier would more than likely go and hide if he wished to survive.

Many people misread this reaction from their dog as 'fear of the correction', rather than fear of the strangers. Many owners believe they have been too hard on their dog by correcting it in this way.

This may lead some owners to feel sorry for their dog and back off on the necessary correction needed to solve the problem. However, they will soon find that this hiding is short-lived. The dog realises that it now has strong leaders and it has no need to hide, as its pack leaders will protect it.

When corrected, fearful dogs usually cease this barking reaction within a few days, providing the owners begin to display strong pack leadership.

Barking during the night

Dogs are naturally more protective at night, because in the wild this is when the pack is more vulnerable. Also, dogs mostly sleep during the heat of the day and become more active in the cool of the evening, when you are least alert. In the wild dogs mostly hunt at night or at dusk, because this is when their prey is more active.

The sounds of normal daytime traffic, pedestrians, factory sounds and all the noises that make up the suburban din to which your dog becomes accustomed seem insignificant to your dog in comparison to the possums, rodents and cats that come out at night and get up to mischief.

Dogs must think that humans are the most inept hunters of all. Here are all of the creatures that they love to chase and the 'boss dog' is curled up in bed, fast asleep. My own dogs just recently spotted a rabbit that crossed our path while out for a bushwalk. They immediately began to chase the rabbit. I growled 'Bah' and they instantly put on the brakes and stopped in their tracks, but they must have thought, 'What can she be thinking? Here is fresh meat on a platter and she doesn't even want to chase it. Some pack leader!' The dog must learn to ignore its natural urges, because our neighbours need their sleep too.

Many people ask me the obvious question, 'How can I be sure that if I stop my dog barking at possums and cats, it will still bark when someone is breaking into the house?' Well, you don't know for sure that it will, but remember that dogs possess a sixth sense, which is most clearly explained in the following case history.

Case history

A Scottish collie named Sandy was a prolific barker. She barked at the broom, the vacuum cleaner, and the lawn mower. With Bark Busters™ therapy and some follow-up treatment from the owners, Sandy was totally cured of barking.

Some months later Sandy's owner rang to tell me that he and his wife were in the house one day when they heard some frantic barking coming from the pool area. They ran to investigate to find the next-door neighbours' two-year-old child sitting on the edge of the pool, with Sandy standing nearby barking at him. The pool cleaner had inadvertently left the gate open.

Sandy's owner said that if that incident had occurred some months earlier, the chances are they would have ignored the barking, thinking it was just Sandy up to her usual nuisance barking.

Though this experience occurred during the day, the same rules apply at night. If your dog is permitted to bark unchecked at everything that moves, it begins to become like the car alarm that goes off constantly. There comes a time when the alarm is ignored and the car thief drives off down the road. In the same way, you will stop checking what your dog is barking at.

The aim should be to cure the nuisance barking, but beyond this, its instinct should prevail when danger is around.

The cure for night barking depends on where your dog sleeps. If it sleeps in your bedroom, then it's easier for you to correct the dog. If your dog sleeps in the laundry, a downstairs area or out in the yard, then the cure will be a little more difficult – you will have to resign yourself to putting in a little more effort.

To solve the barking problem of a dog that is outside or locked up in the garage, you need to practise strong leadership during your waking hours at first. Correct any barking that occurs during the day. Even the barking that occurs when your dog becomes over-excited must be corrected. Follow the instructions in Chapter 10 about walking in and out of doors and from room to room.

Start to display dominant behaviour and your dog will begin to fall into line and become more obedient. Once your dog notices this daily ritual of dominance, you can then begin to correct the barking at night. You will need to employ the Bark Busters™ technique detailed at the end of this chapter. Be sure to catch your dog in the act and praise it the instant it responds.

Confining your dog

Some dogs will calm down, becoming very quiet at night if confined in a secure place such as a portable den, the garage or laundry. This is not always an option as some people will be concerned that they won't have enough protection from burglary. I feel that having my dog inside is far better security than having it running around in the backyard unable to guard against someone coming in the front door.

Having your dog secured, unable to be distracted by all the other creatures running around in the night, is more likely to improve its performance as a guard dog.

Barking at the neighbours

Most of us like to be on good terms with our neighbours. If your dog constantly barks at them, this can cause conflict. If your dog barks at your neighbour each time they walk into their yard, open a door, arrive home from work, mow their lawn and so on, then you need to take action.

If your neighbour is approachable and your dog is generally friendly towards strangers, you might be able to get your neighbours to assist you to fix your dog's barking problem.

Ask your neighbour to walk into their yard, while you work at correcting your dog's behaviour. Use the six-step Bark Busters™ program as detailed opposite.

When your dog is responding reasonably well to your disciplinary actions, more practice will help to cure your dog's barking. Now pretend to go out and hide nearby. Ask your neighbour to again walk into the yard, then wait for your dog to bark at them then step into sight, correcting your dog, and praising it as soon as it responds favourably. You can also go next door and hide, wait to catch your dog barking, then come into sight and correct the barking using the six-step Bark Busters™ program.

17

Basic obedience

The Bark Busters™ six-step correction scale

As dogs have different temperaments, we have developed a six-step correction scale that will ensure that your dog receives the exact type of correction for its personality – no more and no less than the level of correction required to get your dog to respond to your requests.

When correcting your dog's behaviour, always try the softest approach first, working your way up the scale until you have found the right form of correction.

1   The soft growled 'Bah' followed by praise if your dog obeys.
2   The louder growled 'Bah' followed by praise.
3   The soft growled 'Bah' accompanied by a clap.

4   The louder growled 'Bah' accompanied by a louder clap.

5   The soft growled 'Bah' accompanied by the Bark Busters™ 'training pillow'.

6   The louder growled 'Bah' accompanied by the Bark Busters™ training pillow.

If by now you have implemented the dog's language of communication by using the dominant stances and the guttural growls when correcting your dog, then the six-point correction scale is all you will need to show your dog you have the metal to be a strong leader. Also, by doing things such as making your dog move out of your way rather than you having to move out of its way, making it wait until you tell it to eat, and being consistent, you should need no higher level of correction than is indicated on the scale.

Programming

Step 1:

With your dog on a six-foot (1.8m) lead, tell it to sit, while you are holding the lead loosely in your hand. Say 'stay' in your normal speaking voice then step off with one big step, turning to face your dog as you do. If your dog attempts to follow you, growl the 'Bah' word and place your dog back on the spot from which it moved. There is no need for any correction other than the word 'Bah'. Your dog has received his correction and should begin to get the message. Each time it moves, repeat the process until it catches on to what you are trying to get it to do. Be patient, as dogs learn at different rates.

Once you have your dog steady in the 'stay' position, introduce some distractions. See below for information about distractions. Once your dog is reliably staying, then progress to step 2.

Step 2:

With your dog on its lead, walk towards the gate. Correct your dog if it tries to pull ahead or rush through the gate. Have your dog sit just inside the gate while you open it. Persist until it sits patiently while you open the gate. Growl the 'Bah' word each time your dog moves. Once your dog has completed this exercise to your satisfaction, proceed to step 3.

Step 3:

You are now well on your way to having your dog programmed and responsive to the 'Bah' word. Communication with your dog will now become easier.

Now you are ready to try some off-lead control.

Ensure that your yard is secure and that your dog cannot escape by closing all doors to the house and garage. You will need to use the clap technique here or a water squirter or a Bark Busters™ Pillow (available from your nearest Bark Busters™ office, with a lesson). Allow your dog to wander off and investigate. Then when your dog is distracted, call its name in your command voice, saying 'Come!'. Do not allow your dog to disobey your command. It should be turning to respond the instant you call it. If it continues to sniff the ground, then growl the 'Bah' word and either clap loudly or lob your Bark Busters™ training pillow near your dog. Remember to praise your dog the instant it responds, crouching down and then standing as it approaches you.

If your dog is more interested in staying near you, then you might need to introduce some distractions, such as another member of the family. Have them ignore the dog if it runs to them when commanded to come to you. You could also try rolling a tennis ball along the ground, stopping your dog before it reaches the ball, using the clap or Bark Busters training pillow and the 'Bah' word.

Obedience: the basics

Basic obedience is all that most people want from their dog. All that the average person needs or expects is for their dog to come when called, to stay if requested and to be generally well-behaved.

Simple obedience can be taught quite easily with patience as well as consistent use of the correction word 'Bah'.

The recall

This is one of the most important exercises you can teach your dog. A dog that won't come when called can be an embarrassment. If you cannot get your dog to come when called then there is not much else you can do with it. You will be afraid to let your dog off the lead because it won't respond to any command, and if it does escape, a wild chase will ensue.

Case history

The owners of a German Shepherd contacted Bark Busters™ because their dog refused to come when called. As soon as they opened the door to greet the therapist, a large dog appeared from behind them, squeezed past their legs, jumped the front fence and bounded out into the street. His owners immediately gave chase, yelling back at the therapist, 'If we don't catch him, he could be gone for hours!' The therapist called for them to stop. 'What's his name?' he asked the stunned owners, who were now looking at him as if he had two heads.

'His name is Shane.'

The therapist crouched down and in a very high-pitched, sing-song voice called out, 'Here, Shane! Come on, good boy,' patting his legs as he did so. The dog immediately bounded towards him, nearly knocking him flat. Needless to say, the owners stood there in amazement.

Why had the dog come to the therapist, a complete stranger, when it had refused to respond in any way to the owners' calls? They were going about it the wrong way. Firstly they were using the dog's name alone to call it when a dog's name should only be used to attract its attention, because it means nothing to the dog.

Secondly, you should never chase a dog that is running away, because to do so leads the dog to think it's a game or you are all going on a hunt. The calling, to the untrained dog, just sounds like a lot of chatter, similar to the noise dogs make when excited.

If you kneel or crouch, you are adopting a submissive pose, which is more likely to make the dog want to investigate.

Thirdly, the voice tone used is also very important. A harsh tone is not likely to get a dog to approach as it sounds like you are angry. You can use the growl if the dog refuses to come, but the tone must immediately be changed when your dog looks like reacting, to that of a high-pitched sound. Pointing to your feet and screaming in a harsh voice is too threatening for a dog. They will be more likely to want to run the other way.

Finally, Shane's owners were tackling him and grabbing his collar, something that dogs hate with a passion and will make them want to avoid coming anywhere near their owners. This fact is highlighted in the next case history.

Case history

'Gypsy' was a Shetland sheepdog that when asked to 'come', would run around her owner Clara, just remaining out of arm's reach, and avoiding any efforts to grab her. The only way Clara could catch her was to back her into a corner and tackle her 'rugby style'.

All this did was strengthen Gypsy's determination to stay out of reach of her owner when called. Gypsy would only approach to a certain distance and would dart away the instant Clara moved towards her.

When Clara called me in to help, I explained that we had to re-train Gypsy to understand the command 'Come'. We needed to show her that the command did not mean we were going to grab or tackle her.

I spent five minutes lying on the floor (a very submissive, non-threatening position), calling to Gypsy, and finally she came to me. I then spent an hour reprogramming her using a lightweight lead, calling her over and over again and making a fuss of her each time she approached and allowed me to touch her. Through patience and continuous training, I regained her confidence and trust in human hands.

I then got Clara to repeat what I had done. At first Gypsy was not keen to approach her, remembering the old times, but eventually she realised that things had changed.

I checked on Clara and Gypsy a week later, and it warmed my heart to see Gypsy approaching Clara each time she was called, with tail wagging happily. All of her previous fears had gone. Clara had stopped grabbing her and was now praising her each time she approached. Gypsy now had no reason to fear anyone's hands.

These case histories highlight how recall training can become a thing for dogs to fear if not carried out correctly. Your dog must be praised each time it approaches you regardless of how long it takes to get there or how frustrated you feel.

The best way to teach your dog to come when called is to place it on a lightweight lead the way we did with Gypsy. This can then be used to program your dog to respond each time it hears the command 'Come'. You then have the means to ensure it does and providing you praise your dog, there is no reason why it should refuse. Allow your dog to wander off, calling it each time it starts to sniff or investigate. Crouch down as you call it and use a pleasing voice when saying 'Come'.

Drop or stay down

I prefer to use 'drop' as the command for this exercise because it's not used as often in our everyday conversation as the word 'down'. Wherever possible I have used those words not commonly used in everyday speech, to ensure there is no confusion on the dog's part.

'Lie down' command

The 'lie down' command is used for those times when you need your dog to go to its bed or just to go away and lie down. This must firstly be taught while your dog is on lead. This exercise can be conducted either inside the house or outside depending on where your dog spends most of its time.

Find a spot to sit down, allowing your dog to drag the lead. Command your dog to 'lie down' then standing up, lead your dog to a spot away from where you have been sitting and make it lie down. Praise it, wait a second then repeat the process. Each time should be a little longer until you can get your dog to lie down for ten minutes.

Each time, you must be sitting and your dog must be led away and encouraged to lie down, then praised. Repeat this exercise daily. The purpose of the command is to get your dog to go and find a spot to its liking and lie down. It does not need to stay indefinitely, but if it gets up prematurely, you can repeat your command and take it to a spot and make it lie down again.

18

Exercising your dog

There are a lot of theories regarding the essential amount of exercise for a dog. The average dog does not exercise itself regardless of the size of its backyard. Most dogs will just lie down by the back door. When their owner and family become active, so do they, just the way they would react within the pack.

When the pack leader and pack members go for a walk, all other pack members, except very young puppies and nursing mothers, would also go along. It is very unusual for dogs to go walking alone as they much prefer the company of the pack. Only a lack of pack leadership might cause a dog to venture out alone.

I have heard many complaints from dog owners who believe that the size of their dog's backyard is instrumental in whether or not the dog will experience behavioural problems. This is nonsense. We know that dogs do not exercise themselves and the size of the yard, within reason, makes little or no difference to the dog's behaviour, providing that it isn't unreasonably small. Dogs on country properties experience no fewer behavioural problems than dogs that have the run of an average-sized backyard.

All dogs need structured regular exercise to remain fit and healthy. Just as important as physical exercise is mental exercise.

Brains or brawn

Mental exercise can have a direct bearing on solving behavioural problems. Dogs tire much faster when using their brain than they do when running and romping. I witness this daily while visiting dogs in my role as a Bark Busters™ therapist. I always find that the dog is totally exhausted and needs to sleep immediately after the therapy, unlike the dogs that run up to three miles a day with their owners, who tell me they still demolish the backyard.

Exercising your dog's brain is imperative if you want to stave off behavioural problems. Yes! Regular obedience and puzzle toys will provide stimulation for a dog's brain. A dog that does not get mental stimulation will find it hard to concentrate. The brain is a muscle and needs regular use. I have found that it takes much longer to get older dogs (seven to eight years old) to concentrate than younger dogs when they have not had any mental stimulation for so long from their owners.

Summary:

- Physical exercise is important to your dog's fitness.
- Mental exercise is highly beneficial when it comes to solving your dog's behavioural problems and staving off boredom.
- Mental exercise will tire a dog much faster than running it for three miles.

19

Going on holidays

It's a sad but true fact that dogs do not view holidays the way humans do. Dogs react adversely to any change in their routine. Going on holidays for them can be an unpleasant experience. It is inevitable that you will, at some stage, need to board your dog, so this chapter discusses ways of making this experience more pleasant for your dog.

There are ways that you can ensure that your dog does not suffer unduly. As mentioned in Chapter 2, you should ensure that your dog's immunisation is up-to-date if you intend boarding it. The reason for this is that dogs do suffer from stress when taken out of their normal environment. Stress has a way of diminishing the immune system, leaving the dog more susceptible to contracting disease.

The commencement of a daily dose of Vitamin C (ascorbic acid) is also recommended two weeks prior to any boarding to assist in boosting your dog's immune system.

When wild foxes are taken into captivity they have to be immunised immediately against distemper. This is due to the fact that they invariably come down with distemper whenever they are taken into captivity. Stress lowers a fox's natural immunity to disease in the same way that stress affects a dog.

Some people believe that dogs have no need for ongoing immunisation and that there are alternative measures you can take. I urge you to do your own research about this and discuss this matter with a vet.

Having seen how dogs can suffer when their stress levels increase, I will always ensure that my dog is placed on a maintenance program of Vitamin C and immunised prior to boarding it at a kennel.

Selecting a boarding kennel

It is wise to do some research into which boarding kennel to choose for your dog. Do not leave your dog in any establishment that will not allow you to see where your dog will be housed. If you make an appointment to visit a boarding kennel, there should be no reason why you can't be permitted to view the premises.

Factors to consider:

- Will your dog be able to have its own special diet?
- Can the kennel hands administer any special medicine or injections your dog might require?
- Are the kennels clean, secure and warm?

- Are there sufficient exercise facilities?
- Do the kennels have an evacuation plan in case of fire or other natural disasters such as floods and so on?
- Do the kennels have a facility for bathing your dog?

Packing your dog's bags

If the boarding kennel permits, you should pack your dog's favourite bedding and its favourite toys, as well as any special dietary or medical needs.

If permitted, your dog's portable den should also be packed because you will find that your dog will settle in much quicker, and its stress levels will be lower if it is accompanied by familiar items.

Certificates

You will need proof of immunisation before any boarding kennel will accept your dog for boarding. Your vet should be able to supply you with immunisation certificates for your dog's immunisation against distemper, parvovirus and both types of kennel cough.

Home minding

Because of the stress suffered by dogs when away from their natural environment, there is a growing trend to have dogs catered for in their own homes. Some people just ask the next-door neighbour to feed and care for their dog while away on holidays, while others take a more professional approach. They employ a home minding service to care for their dog.

A home minding service is my preferred option whenever I have to go away because my dogs are much happier in their own home.

Although they miss me, their stress levels are dramatically lower than when they are sent away for boarding. The only thing I have to ensure is that the person looking after them is professional. If you choose the home minding option, then check the minder's credentials first.

Things to check:

- Does the home dog minder have a security licence?
- Is the home minder professionally trained to deal with dogs in a kindly, efficient manner and able to handle all situations?
- Does the minder have procedures to cover emergencies such as times when your dog might need a vet?
- Do they record emergency contact telephone numbers?
- Do they have special identification tags for your dog?
- Will they clear the mailbox and water your garden?
- Will they care for your other pets?
- Are they trained to handle emergencies?
- Are they insured?

Once you have found the right home minding service, fit a secure lock to all of your gates and give the minders the keys. This way no unauthorised person will have access to your dog.

Inform your neighbours that you will be away and leave an emergency key, in case of fire, with a trusted neighbour, letting them know that you have arranged for a professional minder for your dog. Leave your contact details with your neighbour as well as the contact number of the minding service.

Then enjoy your holiday!

20

Going to the vet

Many dogs fear going to the vet, especially if the only time they visit a vet is to get an injection. This fear can also transfer to a fear of the car, especially if the only time the dog travels in the car is on a trip to the vet. A journey in the car may then be associated with fear and trauma.

Since a very important part of a dog's life is regular visits to the vet for check-ups, immunisations, worming and so on, you must ensure that there is no fear involved in getting your dog to the vets.

It is wise to do some practice runs to the vet before your dog's visit is due. Prepare some treats for your dog and visit the vet when they are not busy. This will allow your dog to meet the vet and staff. You can use the trip to pick up some worming tablets or to have your dog weighed.

Ask the vet and staff to offer your dog a treat, and then allow some time for him to sniff around and get to know the place.

Whenever your dog has to receive an injection, make sure that you distract it as much as possible with lots of patting while the vet gives the needle. Hold and pat its head. Offering a treat can assist with reducing any future trauma.

Dogs that show aggression to the vet

Some dogs' fear of the vet will manifest itself in aggression. If your dog falls into this category, you will need to ensure that you show it that you do not approve of its anti-social behaviour. Make sure your dog is on lead and that you have full control of its head. Then use the correction word and command and praise your dog when it reacts.

I have found that by holding my hand on a dog's throat I can feel the vibrations if it growls, which is always a precursor to an attack. This then gives me the opportunity to correct the dog while it's still considering attacking the vet, rather than allowing the dog to attack and scare the wits out of all concerned.

Dogs that prove very difficult should be muzzled. Once the dog realises that the vet won't hurt it, they will learn to settle. Muzzling your dog is preferable to wrestling with it, which only creates more stress for the dog.

Summary:
- Have a practice run to the vet some time before your dog's first visit is due.
- Visit the vet at a time when they are not busy.
- Take some treats for your dog so that the vet and other staff can give your dog a treat when they are introduced.
- Discipline any aggressive behaviour and praise your dog when it responds favourably to the discipline.

21

Tips for expectant parents

The moment some people find out they are expecting a new baby, they will go out and buy a new puppy, which is the *last* thing they should do. Having a new puppy is equivalent to having a new baby; it effectively means that they will have two babies, one human, and one canine.

There is a false notion that buying a puppy to coincide with the arrival of a baby ensures that the puppy and baby grow up together. This is a misconception because puppies grow at a much faster rate than a child does.

A labrador puppy at 12 months of age would tower over a one-year-old child, about the same difference between an adult and a horse. So the idea of them growing up together is totally flawed.

The ideal time to get a puppy, if you haven't already got one, is when the child is approaching six years of age. You should preferably choose a small breed of dog. The logic for this is the dog will not outgrow the child and appear like a horse to them.

Proper education of both dog and child are vitally necessary to ensure that future problems do not occur. The dog and child must always be monitored. They need to be taught to respect each other, and this education must come from you.

No child under 12 years of age should be permitted to discipline any dog or puppy. Dogs view children as puppies, which have no pack status. A young child that is permitted to discipline a puppy might one day be bitten by that puppy when it begins to mature.

If you already have a dog when you find out you are about to become a parent, then some important steps need to be followed.

You must start to put in place some initial training to ensure that the transition of introducing your dog to your new baby is done without any danger to the new arrival.

Dogs may react in an adverse way to a new baby. Usually this is the result of a lack of proper introduction on the owners' part or the dog's complete lack of understanding of what a baby is.

Case history

Tara, an expectant mother and the owner of a 12-month-old rottweiler named Zorro, called upon the services of Bark Busters™ recently to assist her with preparing her dog for the arrival of her new baby. She had been warned by her girlfriends to get rid of the dog now that she had a baby on the way. They told her that these types of dogs could not be trusted with children. Tara was very upset at the thought of parting with her beloved Zorro.

We assured her that if the right preparation was carried out, Zorro could live in harmony with her new child.

The first training exercise was to accustom Zorro to a correction word 'Bah' so Tara could communicate to him her dissatisfaction with any undesirable behaviour where the baby was concerned.

We then introduced him to the sounds that babies make. To do this we used a doll that cried like a real baby. We asked Tara to wrap the dolly up like a baby and walk into the lounge room where Zorro was lying down. Tara then activated the baby sound so we could gauge his reaction.

Zorro leapt up, ran at Tara and ripped the doll from her arms. This caught her totally by surprise; she didn't even have time to use her correction word. She looked at us with astonishment.

We explained that this was why we used the pretend baby to educate the dog about how to react to this new experience.

To the untrained eye it appeared that Zorro was indeed a dangerous dog that very well might have harmed Tara's baby. In fact the dog's reaction was quite expected and very normal under the circumstances.

Let's examine the facts from the dog's point of view. The pack leader had entered the room with something in its arms that it had captured. The captured animal suddenly screamed, Zorro leapt into action to assist the pack leader with the capture.

It sounds terrifying, but in the dog's world this is very normal behaviour. We used the crying doll as a way of anticipating what the dog would do when it heard a baby cry so we could see the dog's reaction. This would then allow us to show Tara how to educate Zorro that his behaviour was unacceptable.

The next time the doll's cries were activated, Tara was ready and growled her correction word. Zorro immediately responded and lay down. The pack leader was in control.

We instructed Tara to walk around the house, activating the doll's cries and correcting Zorro until he eventually ignored the cries.

We also suggested some minor changes to Zorro's routine by introducing a portable den for times when Tara might need to leave the baby in its bassinette to peg washing on the line or prepare a meal and so on. We instructed her for safety's sake that when she needed to leave the baby unattended, she was to place Zorro in his portable den, and she could then let him out the instant she returned.

We did not judge him to be a dangerous dog but one with normal reactions that needed guidance as well as good management.

If the right training steps are followed and good management is practised there is no reason why dogs and babies cannot live in harmony.

We must realise that when we share our world with a dog we share it with an animal that lives by a different code to ours. If we keep that utmost in our minds we can learn to live in harmony with dogs.

Summary:
- Introduce the correction word first.
- Practise with a mock baby that cries to ensure you have control before ever introducing your new baby to the dog.
- Introduce a portable den and practise good dog and baby management.

Dealing with dogs' disabilities

Some 35–40 years ago it was very rare to hear of a dog suffering disabilities due to genetics. However, today this is a common occurrence. Increasing numbers of dogs are born blind or deaf. The cause may be emerging genetic problems in modern breeding or it might be that previously these dogs were culled at birth.

Some dogs are born with physical deformities such as hip and elbow dysplasia. These problems are quite common in pure-bred dogs, so much so that reputable breeders now x-ray their breeding stock to ensure they are not carriers of the deformity. The breeders are then issued with a certificate. This does not absolutely guarantee that the offspring of those dogs won't have these problems, but it does reduce the risk when the parents are certified free of the problem.

Hip dysplasia is caused by a rounding off of the hip joint. The causes are not clear but I believe that either indiscriminate breeding or dietary deficiencies are responsible.

Case history

My son Brett bought a rottweiler aged eight weeks from a local breeder. He immediately began feeding his puppy on a natural raw diet. One by one over the next eight months the other puppies from the same litter were all diagnosed with hip dysplasia. The breeder started ringing around to find out how many puppies were actually affected with the problem as the puppy owners were citing poor breeding as the source of the problem. My son's dog turned out to be one of the few puppies that did not have the problem. He was feeding his puppy on a natural diet.

Breeding or diet are not the only causes of dysplasia. It can also be an environmental problem, such as constant running up and down stairs, slipping on tiled floors or even the incorrect carrying of a puppy (where a puppy is carried with its elbows splayed out, rather than supported in a straight position). All of these practices cause problems with the elbow joints as the puppy grows.

Breeding and genetics do have a bearing on dogs being born with joint deformities such as being cow hocked (where the dog's hocks are angled inwards, rather than being straight), having flat pasterns (flat feet), or being pigeon-toed. This is not to say that all breeders are responsible for their puppies being born with these problems. The genetic fault could be from a distant relative whose genes have been passed on down through the generations. Both parents might very well have been physically sound but a dormant gene can surface causing a genetic problem.

Dogs with deformities can live a reasonably happy and long life if special care is taken. The one thing that you must ensure is that a dog with these physical problems is never allowed to breed. These dogs should be desexed to ensure they do not pass on genetic problems to any offspring. You could say this is a necessary part of being a responsible dog owner.

Dogs with disabilities should not be overexercised as you will only add to their discomfort. Overexercising could result in the dog becoming crippled. Small amounts of exercise are fine and even some regular swimming is okay but don't allow your dog to overdo it.

There are dietary supplements you can give to help your dog be comfortable.

Dietary supplements

Certain dietary supplements can have a beneficial effect on some kinds of deformity. A maintenance dosage of Vitamin C (Sodium ascorbate) has been shown to ease the debilitating effects of hip and elbow dysplasia.

Cod liver oil has also been shown to relieve some of the symptoms, making the dog's life a bit easier. It is believed that the oil helps in some way to lubricate the joints, easing the discomfort. It is best to administer the oil on an empty stomach. It should be given gradually at first and then built up to a dessert spoon of oil daily.

There are also medications that assist in easing your dog's discomfort. Discuss this option with your dog's vet.

Any training of a dog with physical disabilities other than hearing or sight impairments must be of a very limited nature. No more than five miutes a day is an appropriate amount, or tailor the exercise to suit your dog's physical capabilities.

Case history

I was asked to fully obedience train a chow chow as its owner was physically handicapped. He needed the dog trained as a companion to accompany him on long walks. On viewing the dog I noticed that it was limping badly in the hindquarters and its general overall disposition was lethargic. I informed the owner that I was unable to commence training with his dog in its present condition.

I also checked the dog's diet and found it was on a very low-grade dog food. I suggested that they detoxify the dog for 48 hours, then start feeding him on a natural raw diet, containing a mixture of raw, meaty bones, raw mince, cod-liver oil and raw fruit and vegetables.

When I returned two weeks later, the dog was jumping out of his skin, his hindquarters were moving freely and his coat was now glossy. I could now get on with the job of training.

Hearing-impaired dogs

As mentioned previously, there are increasing numbers of dogs being born with hearing impairment. This disability tends to strike breeds that have the 'white gene', such as dalmatians, bull terriers, samoyeds, white boxers and some cattle dogs.

White dogs or dogs that are predominantly white tend to be most at risk of being born deaf. There are some people who agonise over whether to keep a hearing-impaired dog or have it put to sleep. I certainly do not believe that there is any good argument for euthanising a deaf dog. Bark Busters™ has successfully trained hundreds of deaf dogs over the years and we have assisted their owners to live in harmony with these otherwise normal dogs. We believe that they make great companions providing their owners are aware of their limitations.

My own dog, Bullseye, lost his hearing before his death. It almost appeared to happen overnight.

Living on a property, I had to quickly implement a technique for communicating with him to ensure he would come quickly when called.

I began using sign language, and being a very intelligent dog, he caught on fast. If he were watching me, there was no problem – he would always respond to my signals and obey my commands. There were problems when he wasn't looking and was heading off down the paddock, totally oblivious to the fact that I was calling him.

I set about devising a plan to get him to look at me when he was away from me, facing the other way. Using a long lead and a torch I taught him to look at me each time I shone the torch beam onto the ground in front of him. This took no time at all, because each time he saw the beam hit the ground, he knew he had to look to me for direction and I would then signal him my command.

When training a hearing-impaired puppy or dog you must be aware

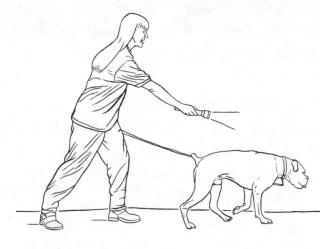

that anything you do needs to be visual. You don't have the convenience of being able to control your dog verbally.

There will be some difficulties at first until you adjust. It is you who will have trouble adjusting because your deaf puppy or dog does not know it is deaf or that it is different to other dogs, so it will have little or no adjustment to make. It's you that will have to understand that you cannot just call out from a distance and have your puppy or dog respond.

However, if special precautions are followed you can learn to enjoy your life with your hearing-impaired pet.

To teach your puppy or dog to respond to visual signals by turning to look at you for direction, train it initially on lead.

Step 1:

Equipment needed: One long lightweight lead, one firm-fitting collar (such as the Bark Busters™ training collar), one Bark Busters™ training pillow (available from your nearest Bark Busters™ office, with a lesson) or small sandbag (made from a piece of rectangular light- coloured material and filled with sand).

Fit the collar and attach the long lead. Allow your dog to wander off on the lead, shine the torch, then lob your Bark Busters™ pillow or sandbag on the ground in the dog's path and where your dog can spot it easily. As soon as you see your dog look at the dropped item, gently tug your dog to get it to turn its head and look at you. Then crouch down and using an inviting signal, gently encourage your dog to come to you.

Repeat several times, ensuring that you wait until your dog/puppy looks at the item before tugging the lead, gently encouraging it to turn and look at you. The article will eventually become a subliminal, visual signal to your dog that says 'Look at me now'.

Be sure to praise with lots of pats the instant it comes to you, then encourage it to stay until you signal that it can leave.

Using torches or laser beams

Torches or laser beams can be very useful for the training of hearing-impaired dogs. They act as a subtle visual sign that has far-reaching capabilities. The dog must be programmed to respond to these signals by first using the long lead, Bark Busters™ training pillow (available from your nearest Bark Busters™ office, with a lesson) and sandbag.

Shine the beam on the ground just ahead of the dog, wait for the dog to spot it, then gently tug the dog so its head turns to look at you.

Warning

Be careful not to shine laser beams into your dog's eyes as this can cause retinol damage. Nor should you encourage your dog to chase the beam, as this can turn into a non-productive game that can make dogs neurotic.

Teaching the sit

Use the same basic method as instructed for hearing dogs, but rather than using the 'sit' command, use a hand signal with your right hand while you place the dog in a sit position with your left hand.

Teaching the stay

This again is executed in the same way as with hearing dogs, only replace the 'Bah' word with a 'stop' signal each time your dog moves, at the same

time flicking the lead in a backward movement in the dog's direction but to the side of the dog rather than into its face. Don't move too far away until your dog gains confidence in the exercise.

Teaching the drop

As with a hearing dog, replace all verbal commands with visual signals that the dog can see. Remember to give praise when your dog responds.

Teaching the 'lie down' command

Just as you would with a hearing dog, point to the place you want your dog to go to and encourage the dog to lie down. Use your 'stop' signal if your dog attempts to move away. Praise the instant it lies down where instructed. Repeat several times. Eventually your dog will learn to go and lie down in the spot you point to.

Eating etiquette

Once again, the procedure is the same as with a hearing dog, but you replace the 'Bah' word with your stop signal (your hand in front of the dog's face) on your dog's lead. Place the food bowl on the ground and, if your dog rushes toward it without a signal from you, then step while you use your visual stop signal.

Training visually-impaired dogs

Where hearing-impaired dogs rely on visual signals, visually impaired dogs rely on sound and scent. Visually impaired dogs need more care and nurturing than hearing-impaired dogs.

Their surroundings should remain constant, such as their kennel, drinking water, food bowls, outdoor furniture and indoor furniture. They should always remain in the same place to ensure that the dog does not become stressed trying to locate its food or water or navigate its territory.

Stairs and dangerous obstacles should be blocked off with child barriers. Attach a small bell to your belt, so your dog can learn to locate you via the sound.

Training a visually impaired dog can be carried out using the 'Bah' word. All commands must be verbal commands.

Care must be taken that the dog does not fall into holes or bump into obstacles. Always attach a lead when going for a walk to ensure you have control over where your dog goes.

I have seen some terrible accidents with sight-impaired dogs, one where a little blind dog fell down a flight of stairs while out on a walk. When the owner finally reached the dog it was at the bottom of the stairs in a shivering mess, its confidence shot to bits.

Summary:

- All signals must be visual and able to be seen clearly by your dog.
- Use the lead to direct your dog to look at you when you drop the visual aid.
- Torches and laser beams make great visual aids, especially at night.
- Teach the 'sit', 'stay' and 'drop' in exactly the same way as you would teach a hearing dog, but always on lead.
- Teach your hearing-impaired dog the correct eating etiquette by stepping on its lead if it moves prematurely.

23

The twilight years

Coping with an aged dog

If your dog has received the correct nurturing and diet, when it reaches an advanced age, its life should not be too different to when it was younger. It will just be a little slower at doing those things it used to bound through in its younger days. Your dog's diet might need to alter at this stage of its life because some aged dogs have problems digesting certain food. Large bones might prove difficult for an older dog to digest and pass through the intestinal tract.

I always alter the diet of my older dogs to a softer kind of food, such as raw chicken wings and raw mince patties, containing cod-liver or flax seed oil, raw fruit, raw veggies and the odd raw egg. My older dogs thrive on this and none of my dogs has ever suffered from arthritis.

I usually make alterations to my dogs' diet when they reach eight years of age. The change is gradual over a period of weeks, when I begin to feed the softer type of food, chicken wings or small meaty, soft rib-type bones.

Keeping them warm

It might be necessary to buy your aged dog a warm doggy coat for the colder months. Dogs naturally carry less muscle and body fat as they age, sometimes lacking the ability to keep themselves warm. Thicker padded bedding might also be necessary, as the lack of body fat does not provide as much cushioning as when they were younger.

Exercise

There is no reason to stop exercising your aged dog altogether, although it will definitely not be able to do the distances nor the pace it did when it was younger. Nature has a way of slowing us all down as we age and dogs are no different.

Playtime

As it ages, your dog might no longer have the tolerance for playing with the children or other dogs, so great care must be taken here to monitor its activities. Some older dogs do not have the patience they used to have. Creaking and arthritic joints can also cause discomfort, especially in the winter months, making the animal less tolerant.

Cod-liver oil added to the diet assists in easing the debilitating pain of arthritis. There are also some medications available from your vet for the treatment of arthritis.

Case history

Bark Busters™ was called in to treat a case of sibling rivalry between a young Staffordshire terrier and an ageing Jack Russell terrier. The two dogs had suddenly taken to fighting each time they saw each other. The problem was upsetting the owners, who could not believe the change in their pet's behaviour.

The two dogs had always romped and played together, so this new behaviour was totally out of character.

We immediately identified the problem. The older dog had become arthritic and was moving quite stiffly, so it was obvious that the rough play by the younger dog was adding to its problems.

The Jack Russell, mindful of the pain the younger dog would inflict on it during play, was having none of it and would instead attack the Staffordshire terrier as it approached.

The Staffordshire terrier, oblivious to why this was occurring, would retaliate and a ferocious fight would ensue.

It was sad, but we had to instruct the owners to stop the 'playtime'. These two dogs were going to have to find different ways to interact with each other.

Ageing brings many changes

An ageing dog goes through many changes, so you will need to monitor the progression carefully. A slight loss of hearing can occur as dogs age. It may begin with an inability to hear the lower tones. For example, your dog might begin to ignore your normal speaking voice yet respond to your higher pitched sounds. This selective hearing is a form of hearing loss that naturally occurs as your dog ages.

Deterioration of your dog's hearing might lead to complete loss of hearing as it ages.

Other changes may include the dog's eyesight begining to fade. This can be due to cataracts forming on the eye. You can check for this yourself by inspecting your dog's eyes. If your dog has cataracts you will see a cloudy looking film partially covering the eye. Cataracts affect the dog's vision, sometimes leading to blindness. Speak to your vet about possible cures, keeping in mind the age of the dog and whether it is wise to pursue any radical surgery at this stage of your dog's life.

As these changes occur gradually in ageing dogs most dogs learn to cope reasonably well. As long as you adjust to the dog's needs, there should be no problems.

Other dogs in the household, especially younger ones, might need to be separated from the older one to allow your aged dog much-needed rest or to prevent problems occurring.

Cases of fights occurring in households of two dogs is very high where one of the dogs is aged and is losing its hearing, sight or both, as described in the following case history.

Case history

Bonnie and Clyde, two Welsh corgis, had always been inseparable. Even though Bonnie was four years younger than Clyde, their relationship had stood the test of time. That was until Clyde began to lose his sight and hearing. The changes were gradual. At first the owners noticed minor squabbles and thought nothing of it. These squabbles finally turned into all-out battles, where one dog would end up being taken to the vets for repairs to ripped ears and so on.

Their owners, Janine and Stuart, were determined that they would keep the two dogs together. They had, after all, been together for years without any problems, so why would things change now? The fights continued. In desperation they called Bark Busters™ in to treat the problem.

We ran some tests to check for deafness and suspected that Clyde was completely deaf. We also noticed cataracts on both eyes and sensed that if he did have any sight, it was possibly negligible. A quick visit to the vet confirmed our findings. It was also discovered that Janine had inadvertently cut back on Clyde's arthritis medication about a month before the fights started.

We explained to Janine and Stuart that Clyde's disabilities – his deafness, loss of sight as well as some arthritic pain – had grave implications for his interaction with Bonnie. Previously Bonnie had been in the habit of letting Clyde know that he was out of line, quite typical behaviour from a female dog. She would do this by the use of body language and guttural growls. In the past Clyde would back off with any unwanted amorous moves and would go about his business.

However, as he aged Clyde could no longer see or hear her signs of disapproval and she would then escalate the discipline to the next level – attack. Totally oblivious to her distaste of his approaches, Clyde would think she was attacking him for no reason and would retaliate.

Clyde's medication was reintroduced. Bonnie and Clyde were only allowed to be together and interact when their owners were around. We introduced a water squirter, which was used to stop Bonnie from attacking Clyde. Hearing-impaired training was carried out for Clyde using the torch beam, so Clyde would stop what he was doing and focus on his owners for direction.

24

Dealing with the loss of a dog

The saddest thing about owning a dog is the fact that dogs don't live very long. People who love dogs will own many dogs in their lifetime and will have to suffer the loss of a beloved pet many times.

My husband Danny once said to me that he believes the reason that dogs do not live very long is to allow us to own many wonderful dogs in our lifetime. He believes when a dog dies it is to make room for another wonderful dog to come into our life. This thought has eased my pain more than once in the past when I have lost one of my dogs through old age.

Whichever way you look at it, the loss of a dog is not easy to take. People cope differently with loss. Some people like to go out and get another dog immediately, while others say they will never get another dog. I can understand that people who feel a loss will want to take action in order to cope with their grief.

I believe that all dogs go to heaven and that we will eventually meet up with our dogs in the afterlife. This helps me cope with the loss of my beloved pets. The thought that I will again see my dearly departed dogs makes the pain of their passing bearable.

Some people find the loss of a pet so unbearable that they go to the length of having their animals stuffed and preserved for all time. I much prefer to take pictures or commission a painting, as I believe this preserves the memory of a loved pet much better. We all have different ways of coping.

I have found that getting out the old photos and watching the videos helps me, even though it's painful and I shed many tears. I believe this is all part of the grieving process and it helps to celebrate their life rather than mourn their passing.

Making the final decision

There have been several times in the past when I have had to make the unenviable decision to have an ailing dog put to sleep. There are some people who argue that nature should be allowed to take its course, leaving the animal to die of natural causes.

This is very honourable thinking, but sometimes nature's way is a very slow and cruel way. I guess the same people would argue that this is nature's way of slowly preparing the animal for death, which will come eventually but should not be rushed.

I know it's not an easy decision and I believe it should be left to the person who knows the dog best, as they are the ones who can determine if the dog has quality of life. Although disabled, some dogs will still enjoy their life and should not be put to sleep just because they are old.

My own bull terrier gave us many scares during his final days when each day we thought we would have to make the decision but then he would rally. This went on for weeks until one sleepless night, I believed he was asking for an end to the torment. He came and laid his soft, milky-white head in my lap and I could feel his strength waning. He needed me to be strong for him, so I made the decision that night. The vet confirmed the next morning that the decision was the right one.

I honestly believe that watching a pet's suffering makes this decision about putting a pet to sleep easier, because we cannot bear to see our loved ones suffer.

If you find yourself in the unenviable position of having to put a beloved pet to sleep, make sure that you summon the strength to stay with that pet when the time comes and see it through. During my days at the RSPCA I was always saddened when I was left with someone's adored pet during euthanasia to give it the solace it needed from the one who loved it most.

Bark Busters™ 50 most popular breeds

There are hundreds of wonderful breeds of dogs in the world, all with special attributes. The breeds mentioned here are Bark Busters™ 50 most popular breeds according to our records. The majority of these breeds are also amongst some of the easiest breeds to train. The easiest breeds to train are rated five stars and those harder to train are marked in stars in descending order of number.

Airedale ★★★
Australian cattle dog ★★★★★
Australian shepherd ★★★★★
Australian terrier ★★★
Bearded collie ★★
Bichon frise ★★★★★

Border collie ★★★★★

Boston terrier ★★★★

Bull terrier ★★

Cairn terrier ★★★

Cavalier King Charles ★★★★★

Chihuahua ★★

Clumber spaniel ★★★

Corgi ★★★

Cross breeds of all description ★★★★★

Dachshund (long haired) ★★★★

Doberman ★★★★★

English springer ★★★

Field spaniel ★★★

Flat-coated retriever ★★★★

French bulldog ★★★★

German coolie ★★★★

German shepherd ★★★★★

German shorthaired pointer ★★★

Golden retriever ★★★★★

Greyhound ★★★★★

Hungarian vizsla ★★★★

Italian greyhound ★★★★★

Jack Russell ★★

Kerry blue ★★★

Labrador retriever ★★★

Large Munsterlander ★★★★★

Miniature pinscher ★★★

Nova Scotia duck tolling retriever ★★★★

Pomeranians ★★★★

Poodle ★★★★★

Pug ★★★

Rottweiler ★★★★★

Rough collie ★★★★★

Samoyeds ★★

Schipperke ★★★

Schnauzer ★★★★★

Shetland ★★★★★

Siberian husky ★★★

Skye terrier ★★★★

Staffordshire terrier ★★★★

Tibetan spaniel ★★★

Welsh springer spaniel ★★★

West Highland ★★★★

Whippet ★★★★★

Please note:

The labrador retriever has been given only a three-star rating in our list, due to the fact that some of the labrador retrievers are becoming extremely difficult to train because of indiscriminate breeding. If this is your choice of dog, be sure to source your puppy from a reputable breeder that has been breeding for temperament over many years.

26

Bark Busters™ canine personality profile

Circle the rating that best applies, and total the points below:

1.	When the doorbell rings, does your dog bark and/or run to the door?	I	5	10
2.	Does he seek attention by asking to be petted or to play?	I	5	10
3.	Does your dog jump up on visitors (and sometimes on you)?	I	5	10
4.	Does your dog ignore you when you call him to come?	I	5	10
5.	Does your dog exhibit destructive behaviours, i.e., ruining furniture, etc.?	I	5	10
6.	Does your dog lunge at other dogs or people when on a walk?	I	5	10
7.	Does your dog toilet or mark in the house?	I	5	10
8.	Does he chew on items such as shoes, kids' toys, trash, etc.?	I	5	10

9.	Does your dog play too aggressively with children?	I	5	10
10.	Does your dog bark at the fence, passers-by, or just anything?	I	5	10
11.	When left alone, does your dog show signs of 'separation anxiety'?	I	5	10
12.	Does your dog show any symptoms of allergies?	I	5	10
13.	Is your dog very anxious and/or more aggressive at the vet hospital?	I	5	10
14.	Does your dog 'steal' items, such as food, from counters or tables?	I	5	10
15.	When in a 'stay', does he leave the stay before being released?	I	5	10
16.	Does your dog show any aggression toward other dogs?	I	5	10
17.	Does your dog run up the stairs and/or through doors ahead of you?	I	5	10
18.	Does he walk ahead of you, or pull you when on the leash?	I	5	10
19.	Does your dog become anxious in the car by barking or pacing?	I	5	10
20.	Has your dog ever bitten a person or another dog? If so, circle 10.			10

Add columns: _____

Total points: _____

Transfer the points from the previous page into the appropriate space below. Then, write the letter grade on the line provided. For example, a rating of 30 equates to a B+, while a rating of 95 would receive a D. Estimate the letter grade as best you can.

19–27	28–50	51–85	86–139	140–200
+ A –	+ B –	+ C –	+ D –	+ F –

Grade

(Your dog's name) letter grade: _____

Grade A: This dog is extremely well behaved. Congratulations!

Grade B: Dogs in this category are typically wonderful family dogs with a few rough edges. This dog could easily move to the 'A' group with some training.

Grade C: While these dogs need training, usually they don't receive it because their annoying behaviours 'are just not bad enough'. It's unfortunate, because 'C' dogs can be wonderful pets, and bring great joy and happiness to families. And, with training, the owner can be assured the behaviour will only improve.

Grade D: This category of dogs has issues that can be serious if not addressed soon. Owners of these dogs are constantly being annoyed and irritated by their behaviour, and are beginning to think, 'Something has got to be done'. Fortunately, dogs can change their behaviour quite easily, so these owners should seek help immediately.

Grade E: Most people with dogs that rate an 'E' are desperate for change, but many don't know what to do. These dogs are 'out of control', and serious problems can arise if they are not trained. Owners of these dogs sometimes consider putting them down. However, the vast majority of dogs can be saved with training, eliminating the owner's grief and guilt.

Index

Bark Busters™ Offices

Australia
Tel: 1800 067 710

New Zealand
Tel: 0800 167 710

United Kingdom
Tel: 0808 100 4071

United States
Tel: 1877 280 7100

Canada
Tel: 1866 418 4584

Japan
Tel: 0120 272 109

Bark Busters™ Website
www.barkbusters.com

Bark Busters™ have franchises available worldwise, seeking people who love dogs and those who want to make a difference to the lives of man's best friend.

Recommended Reading

Billinghurst, I., *Give Your Dog a Bone*, Ian Billinghurst, 1993.
Billinghurst, I., *Grow Your Puppy with Bones*, Ian Billinghurst, 1993.
Billinghurst, I., *The BARF Diet*, Ian Billinghurst, 1993.
Lonsdale, T., *Raw Meaty Bones Promote Health*, Rivetco Pty Ltd, 2001.
Schultze, K., *Natural Nutrition for Dogs and Cats: The Ultimate Diet*, Hay House.

All books listed above are available from:
PO Box 703
Lithgow NSW 2790

The author with Bullseye.